Gender Responsive Justice

At the end of the twentieth century a step-change in thinking about the offending behaviour of women began to impact on policy-makers concerned with the treatment of female offenders. A growing number of nations, states and organisations both national and supra-national in nature began to acknowledge that existing criminal justice and especially penal practices had not been sufficiently attentive to women's needs and had discriminated against women as a result.

The concept of 'gender-responsive justice' – an orientation to working with women and girls based around a consideration of the special needs of women as prisoners and their particular pathways to offending – has been developed as a result. This book explores the development of this concept, the theories which have informed it, policy arenas in which gender-responsive justice has been attempted and the practices of gender-responsive justice which have subsequently emerged. This book takes a global perspective as it outlines the different international and national arenas within which gender-responsive justice gained favour and considers what has been learned from this novel and feminist-inspired approach.

Gender-responsive justice has not been without its critics, however, and this book also examines the different arguments which have been used to attack or critique the concept from varied perspectives. This book lays down a clear theoretical framework for understanding gender-responsive justice and will be useful in assessing current and future policy-making in this area.

Karen Evans is a senior lecturer in the Department of Sociology, Social Policy and Criminology at the University of Liverpool, UK. Karen has published, researched and taught in the area of Gender and Crime for more than ten years.

Routledge Critical Studies in Crime, Diversity and Criminal Justice

Edited by Sharon Hayes, University of Newcastle, Australia
Patricia Faraldo Cabana, University of A Coruña, Spain

The works in this series strive to generate new conceptual and theoretical frameworks to address the legal, organisational and normative responses to the challenges that diversity and intersectionality present to criminal justice systems. This series aims to present cutting-edge empirically informed theoretical works from both new and established scholars around the world.

Drawing upon a range of disciplines including sociology, law, history, economics and social work, the series encourages different approaches to questions of mobility and exclusion with a cross-section of theorists, empiricists and critical policy researchers. It will be key reading for scholars who are working in criminal justice, criminology, criminal law and human rights, as well as those in the fields of gender and LGBTI studies, migration studies, anthropology, refugee studies and post-colonial studies.

1. Gender Responsive Justice
A Critical Appraisal
Karen Evans

Gender Responsive Justice

A Critical Appraisal

Karen Evans

Routledge
Taylor & Francis Group
LONDON AND NEW YORK

First published 2018 by Routledge

2 Park Square, Milton Park, Abingdon, Oxfordshire OX14 4RN
52 Vanderbilt Avenue, New York, NY 10017

Routledge is an imprint of the Taylor & Francis Group, an informa business

First issued in paperback 2019

British Library Cataloguing in Publication Data
A catalogue record for this book is available from the British Library

Library of Congress Cataloging in Publication Data
Names: Evans, Karen, 1961- author.
Title: Gender responsive justice : a critical appraisal / Karen Evans.
Description: Abingdon, Oxon ; New York, NY : Routledge, 2017. |
Series: Routledge critical studies in crime, diversity and criminal justice ;
1 | Includes bibliographical references and index.
Identifiers: LCCN 2017005713 | ISBN 9780415372244 (hardback) |
ISBN 9781315231310 (ebook)
Subjects: LCSH: Female offenders. | Criminal justice, Administration of. |
Feminist criminology.
Classification: LCC HV6046 .E93 2017 | DDC 364.3/74--dc23
LC record available at https://lccn.loc.gov/2017005713

ISBN: 978-0-415-37224-4 (hbk)
ISBN: 978-0-367-22721-0 (pbk)

Typeset in Times New Roman
by Taylor & Francis Books

To Eileen and Crawford

Contents

Acknowledgements

This is a book which has been a number of years in its making. It has been germinating since 2009 when I was invited to join a team of researchers based at London South Bank University who had been engaged by the UK Ministry of Justice to evaluate the pilot of a gender-specific disposal – the women's conditional caution, sponsored by the then Solicitor General for the Labour Government, Vera Baird. It was my honour and delight to conduct interviews with women who had accepted such cautions and the staff with whom they were engaged in working inside Together Women's Centres across the North West of England. So, my thanks to Marisa Silvestri, Helen Easton and Roger Matthews for making this experience possible. How times have changed in the period since!

I would also like to thank Belinda Carpenter and Kerry Carrington who allowed me to spend two periods of study in Australia based at QUT, Brisbane, attached to their department and the Crime and Justice Research Centre. I would particularly like to thank Belinda and her family for hosting me in their home until I could find more permanent accommodation. I couldn't have done it without you. I have to thank too Kim and Peter Kaim, Clancy and Tayo whom I finally ended up lodging with and Tayo especially for introducing me to the artistry and insights of Kendrick Lamar. I would also like to extend my gratitude to Molly Dragiewicz who took time to watch whales with me and take me to the beach, and to all the staff at QUT who supported me when I was so far away from home.

And as for my home, thanks once again to the indomitable Dave. I was away from you for too long – we will be closer together in the future.

Introduction

Throughout most of history women have been largely subjected to the same punishments as men. Whether punishment involved a focus on the body as a site of discipline, the shift to incarceration, transportation, the removal of the offending body from society or the more welfare- and 'treatment'-related models which were developed in the twentieth century, inhabiting a female body has been said to have made little to no difference to practices of punishment (White 2014:284). Those theories which have been developed to justify the chosen punishment regime in any given period have been formulated without apparent consideration as to the differing effects which forms of punishment may have on any particular social group. Indeed a universality in the offending person has been assumed so that punishment has been considered as equally applicable and appropriate for all to whom it is meted out. In all other aspects of the legal system however, principles of universality have not been applied. Clear distinctions have been made as to the legal rights enjoyed by different social groups across society, with many minorities and the entirety of the female sex denied many of the rights enjoyed universally by the male. Still, even without access to the same legal, political and social rights as her male counterparts, theories of punishment have not singled the female out for any special attention. Women have been accorded an equal responsibility to act in accordance with the rule of law, however discriminatory it may be in practice and however much it might work in opposition to their interests, and to face any subsequent punishment.

It was not until the 1980s that scholars began to take a serious and sustained interest in the gendered experiences of punishment and criminal justice. Their research revealed that women's relationship to the law, their motivations for law-breaking and the consequent impact on their lives of being labelled as offenders were in many ways profoundly dissimilar to those of men. These scholars, mainly feminist in their standpoint, began to raise significant questions as to the suitability of 'man-made law' (Naffine 1990) to the lives of women and girls. Whilst systems of 'justice' and regimes of punishment have often proved to be both physically and psychologically harmful to *all* those sentenced, these theorists argued that women and girls, whilst travelling through the same processes of punishment as men and boys, had been and continued to be subjected to particular humiliations and suffering which were not shared by their male counterparts. By the 1990s this concern had grown to such an extent that some feminist scholars began to call for a redrawing of the law and of punishment regimes in order to take into consideration the very different circumstances in which women experienced the criminal justice system. By the turn of the century the concepts of *gender-specific justice* and later *gender-responsive justice* had been formulated and proposed as a necessary part of any system of criminal justice which claimed parity of treatment for both sexes.

This book traces the development of the concept of gender-responsive justice and critically explores its applications since the 1990s. As a result the book focuses on the workings of the criminal justice system and ways in which the concepts of gender-specific and gender-responsive justice have been applied to women who have come into contact with the criminal justice system as law-breakers. Of course the idea of 'justice' is much wider than this focus on 'the offender' and it can, and should, be considered as applicable to many other aspects of women's lives; however, the concept of gender-specific justice with which this book is concerned was originally formulated as a response to the harms meted out to women within systems of criminal, rather than social, justice and it is for this reason that this book will follow that original concern. Later chapters, however, will begin to address some of the wider issues which the concept of gender-specific/responsive justice raises outside the narrow confines of the criminal justice system.

In this book I use the somewhat cumbersome terms 'women who break the law' or 'female law-breakers' in preference to the usual terms employed within mainstream criminology – those of 'offenders' or 'criminals'. I use these alternative terms because female bodies have caused 'offence' in mainstream society for all sorts of reasons – when women assert their rights, when they assert their sexuality and when they do not play by the 'normal' rules – and so the term sits very uncomfortably with me. I also eschew use of the terms 'offender' and 'criminal' as representing labels which women who have broken the law wholeheartedly reject as stripping them of their identities as women and imposing punitive logics on their bodies and selves which they feel are often inappropriately applied to their particular circumstances, motivations and actions. As a sometime law-breaker myself (details of which I will withhold in this instance) I also reject the term 'criminal' as my own experiences have demonstrated that sometimes personal actions which break the current laws of the land can be personally and politically justifiable. In addition, in this book I refrain from speculating on or making judgements about the morality of women's law-breaking but take a more abstracted view on punishment and its purposes and effectiveness.

The book takes a long view on punishment and its [mis]appropriation and at various feminist-inspired movements to reimagine and reconstruct regimes of punishment along more egalitarian lines. Chapter 1 explores the development of punishment in practice and in theory and reveals the masculinist nature of the logics and assumptions which underpin the punishment regimes which we largely accept today. It reveals women's experiences have been ignored and rendered insignificant but in addition argues that an underlying and overwhelming misogyny in the frameworks of punishment has gone unremarked. The chapter explains that it took the blossoming of second-wave feminism and its interventions into the subject from the late 1960s before any serious account of the punishment of females was attempted. The remainder of the chapter considers this writing out of women and explores the early attempts of feminists to put right this wrong and to challenge masculinist accounts of the place which punishment has held in societies both contemporary and past.

Chapter 2 then considers the intervention of females into criminology and criminal justice practice in the latter part of the twentieth century. The early reformers were liberal reformists, concerned with improving the experiences of women as a necessary and social good and with raising the issue of women's right to fair and decent consideration of their particular needs and driven by compassion towards women, and their children, but their vision could not encompass a critique of the masculinist frameworks of knowledge and understanding. Once the values and methods of second-wave feminism were brought to the attention of criminology these began to make an impact into the ways in which this more critical section of the discipline considered and operationalised its key concepts. Women were introduced to the discipline as victims and as offenders and prominent feminists proposed that a wholesale transgression of criminology's boundaries was needed before the discipline could become sensitive to gender and its impact on behaviour.

The rise of gender-specific justice practices is discussed in Chapter 3. The late twentieth century was a remarkable period for the growth of knowledge and interest in the lives of girls and women. In the development of women as a legitimate area of study we see the initial phase of thinking which was to lead to the call for a sensitivity to gender in policy and practice. The serious exploration of women's lives brought to global attention the multifaceted oppression which women face as women and which is specific to the workings of gendered social relations. The chapter discusses the move to develop 'women-centred', 'gender-aware' and 'gender-specific' criminal justice programmes for women and then turns to the idea of 'gender-responsive' practices which emerged in the 1990s. It argues that these latter approaches may have moved the subject of punishments for women into more mainstream penal logics.

In more recent years as the call for gender-responsive justice has begun to be heard there have been calls to explore gender as an issue for men and boys too. Chapter 4 explores the evolution of this idea, explaining in more detail the female-focus of the debate and considering the different arguments which have been put forward which support or reject the call for an expansion of gender-responsive justice so that it incorporates the experiences of men and boys. It reveals also that gender-responsive justice has come under sustained criticism from conservative forces in society such as the men's rights movement.

Chapter 5 looks at criticisms of gender-responsive justice which flow from more radical and critical perspectives. First to be discussed are critiques which have been inspired and constructed from a feminist perspective – many of which are largely sympathetic to the ideals of gender-responsive justice, but feel that it has been poorly executed – then the latter part of the chapter explores critiques which have been more hostile to the idea of gender-responsive justice, either because they believe that the focus on gender is either problematic or partial or because they take more radical positions which seek to transform penal regimes beyond the boundaries of gender-responsive approaches.

The final chapter returns to a discussion of the fundamental arguments which have been made to underpin the development of woman-centred, gender-specific and gender-responsive justice which have been developed over a number of decades and have changed in their emphasis and tone during this period. It concludes that it is not enough for us to reveal the discriminatory and harmful practices which penal systems based on androcentric principles have imposed on the female body and mind. While practices of punishment and justice have been exposed by feminist arguments which have impacted on the delivery of many aspects of the criminal justice system, it is not enough to tinker with systems which have already been revealed as fundamentally damaging, destructive and toxic to those who come under their purview. It is important that we look again at developing systems of justice which are based around more inclusive, progressive and international perspectives and which include a resistance to current practices rather than an accommodation to them.

References

Naffine, N. (1990) *Law and the Sexes: Explorations in Feminist Jurisprudence*. London: Allen and Unwin.

White, W.L. (2014) 'Advocacy for gender specific addiction treatment and recovery support: an interview with Dr. Stephanie Covington', www.williamwhitepapers.com/pr/2014%20Dr.%20%20Stephanie%20Covington.pdf [Accessed 2 March 2016].

Chapter 1

Man made punishment

While claims as to the universal nature of the law and its equal applicability across society have been challenged by many philosophers across the ages, theories of punishment have not been held up to the same scrutiny. Penal theory has, in the main, considered how society should rightfully and justifiably respond to an offending act but in the goal to develop regimes of penality there has been little reflection on the unequal distribution of power and agency within the societies in which practices of punishment operate. Liberal theories have considered the threat of punishment as a deterrent necessary for the maintenance of social order without questioning the nature of that order which is to be sustained and the manner in which it may be differently constituted for various social groups. Retributive practices have based their argument on a moral judgement, that punishment is a justified response to a wrongdoing which should reflect the harm of the crime committed, without a consideration of the ways in which morality is both differently applied and policed across society. While the nature of and rationalisations for punishment have undergone significant paradigmatic shifts over the centuries, each system has been considered as germane to all members of the society in which it has been applied and considered as the most apposite method through which all those who have been wronged can be afforded some sort of redress. There has been little room in these different conceptions of punishment and its utility for a consideration as to how practices of punishment may be differentially experienced or understood by the law-breaker themself, or indeed as to how punishment may be more or less effective for different social groups. The rules and justifications for different models of punishment have been considered as universal systems which should be applied to all.

The punishment models which we currently utilise in order to frame our response to law-breaking were developed prior to the formation of critical theories such as feminism which have highlighted the unequal distribution of rights across societies. Established and centuries-old theories of punishment have become deeply entrenched into our ways of thinking about and practising punishment and in justifying the right to punish. These established approaches suggest that punishment is located outside of and above the messy structures of everyday life and that the principles on which punishment is based constitute universal truths. Indeed for many these truths have been decreed by a higher power, whether that be earth-bound or heavenly, with a paternal concern to ensure a better society for all. Punishment is accepted as a constant in society and as based on a system of morals which supersede the day-to-day exercise of authority and which ultimately hold us all to account whatever our position in society, regulating the behaviour of all on equal terms. We are, as a society, less familiar with the more critical and complex understandings of punishment which have more recently emerged over the last 100 or so years and which have called for a new approach to our understanding of punishment (see discussions of Marx, Nietzsche, Foucault and Menninger in Tunick 1992). These radical critiques have considered punishment as linked to extant social conditions, less a response to crime than an expression of social and economic power and its maintenance. Punishment regimes have been reconceptualised as systems through which the powerful maintain their hold over society and find justification in their reproach and censure of ideas and individual actions which threaten the maintenance of power, and which also hold the powerful to a different set of standards than those which are applied to the powerless (Tunick 1992).

The development of punishment in practice and in theory has missed numerous opportunities to include the perspectives of women. As a consequence the theory and practices which have been developed have been masculinist in the extreme; not only have women's experiences been ignored but an underlying and overwhelming misogyny has gone unremarked. As we will see in the following exploration of punishment over the centuries, it took the blossoming of second-wave feminism and its interventions into the subject from the late 1960s before any serious account of the punishment of females was attempted. The remainder of this chapter considers this writing out of women and later turns to the early attempts by feminists to put right this wrong and to challenge masculinist accounts of the place which punishment has held in societies, contemporary and past.

The privatisation of punishment for women and girls

Systems of punishment, while they reflect the dominant cultures and beliefs held within society in any particular period, are also influenced by a society's traditions and customs and they must be understood in their historical as well as their current social context. Furthermore punishment plays a significant part in the more general and widespread apparatus of social control which exists in any society and reflects the extant economic and social relations which are played out in both the public and private spheres (Garland 2001, Hudson 2003). Nietzsche was an early critic of punishment, which he revealed as a social practice. In his 1887 essay *On the Genealogy of Morals* Nietzsche considered punishment, not as a fundamental moral response to harm, but as a way in which the powerful could exercise and enjoy their control over others whom they considered to be beneath them and subject to their authority (Tunick 1992:21). Modern theories of punishment claim to have rationalised and regulated mechanisms of social control in society in order to eradicate the abuses of power which characterised the punishment regimes of autocratic pre-modern and pre-democratic societies. In many ways, however, they have failed in this endeavour, integrating instead the discriminatory practices of former ages into what are considered modern and egalitarian forms of punishment. While the form and seat of power may have shifted somewhat, members of less powerful social groups are still subject to markedly differing degrees and types of disciplinary control than those played out across society as a whole. As Foucault (1979) observed, the power to punish is not solely located within the key institutions of the justice system but is equally found inside family and neighbourhood and within the dynamics of our most intimate relationships. A combination of historical and discriminatory practices and beliefs as well as the everyday pervasive and pernicious control of the female sex has placed women in a particularly invidious position when it comes to the willingness of society to punish what have been considered their deviant acts. These cumulatively reinforcing mechanisms which play out at all levels of society explain the eagerness with which particular forms and levels of discipline have been, and continue to be, disproportionately applied in order to control the behaviour of women and girls.

Women and girls have suffered detriment in multiple ways. They have historically been considered of less economic and social value than have men and boys and as a consequence less care was taken over their safety and security (Newman 1978). In addition the punishment of females has often been handed over to the father or husband so that sentence could be privately administered, ensuring that the family was not publicly shamed by her guilt. One consequence of the surrendering of punishment to the private arena of the family has been the absence of a public regulation and scrutiny of the punishment of women in the home – a problem whose legacy is all too evident today and is played out in the private beatings and coercive controls to which many women are still subjected within their familial and intimate relationships. The female sex continues to bear the responsibility for upholding the moral standing and honour of the family, with transgression subject to severe punishment, even to the extent of 'honour killings' which are nothing short of femicide, where individual women are found to have fallen short in this task, their guilt firmly established and punishment enacted outside of systems of public justice (Carrington 2015). The privatisation of the punishment of women and girls has been institutionalised both through the enactment of laws which have sanctioned this relationship and through the censures placed on the behaviour of women and girls through more informal, often family-based, moral injunctions.

By the Middle Ages, Newman (1978) argues, the law was increasingly institutionalised into public life which meant that women were more often brought into public systems of censure and were sentenced and punished alongside men. Rather than achieving parity in their treatment however, the discriminatory, and publicly approved, privatised practices of the past endured alongside this entry of women into systems of public justice. So while records for this period show fewer women were brought to trial than men – a ratio of one to every nine men – this did not signal an improvement in the treatment of women, as Newman (1978:57) suggests. Newman makes a number of errors in this proposition which have since been often repeated; first the error of measuring the control of women only in terms of formal systems of punishment and sanction and then to assume that formal institutions afford everyone who comes before them the same respect and impartial judgement. The inclusion of women who break the law into formalised systems of justice only added another layer to their control in society which institutionalised former practices of patriarchal power. The double burden of parallel and mutually reinforcing systems of punishment has been devastating in its impact on the female sex but this has largely gone unremarked. The evidence, however, is all too clear. Women who killed their husbands, for example, were likely to be charged with treason as they had killed their 'lord' and superior. Females who killed spouses were consequently more likely to receive the death penalty whereas men would be judged to different standards and receive a range of penalties, many of which would be much less severe. Indeed, men who killed women could be completely exonerated and their actions considered justified in various ways (Newman 1978). The institutionalisation of patriarchal practices further robbed women of their agency and severely punished them for stepping outside of accepted behavioural norms. Within the family they remained subject to the controlling hands of husbands and fathers who were supported in their violence by the law for many centuries. Indeed it could be argued that, in the current disproportionate violence to which women are subjected in the private sphere, these earlier accepted forms of discriminatory punishment still apply to women in the home today. In addition it is only in recent history that legislation has been amended in some countries to outlaw the privatised punishment of women and girls and to afford the female sex a measure of equal treatment by the law.

The silencing of women

Western justice systems have been profoundly influenced by early Christian teachings within which women have been afforded a subordinate role. Within these scriptures, written largely by men, are many examples where women's voices have been subjugated and wherein women have been advised to remain submissive subjects of their male relatives. Men, by contrast, were charged with the education of women and with the policing of their behaviour as the following quote reveals:

> The women should keep silent in the churches. For they are not permitted to speak, but should be in submission, as the Law also says. If there is anything they desire to learn, let them ask their husbands at home. For it is shameful for a woman to speak in church.
>
> (1 Corinthians 14:34–35, ESV)

Christianity has also included the significant and recurrent trope of the female sex as dangerous to men, casting woman as the powerful temptress who can bring men down to base and sinful ways. Men are enjoined to be wary of the power of female sexuality and to subject women's appearance and behaviour to tightly limited restrictions as a consequence. To ensure women do not bring men into disreputable behaviour the female sex was trained to be demure and chaste, to stay within the bounds of domesticity and respectability and to pass these 'virtues' on to succeeding generations:

> Older women likewise are to be reverent in behaviour, not slanderers or slaves to much wine. They are to teach what is good, and so train the young women to love their husbands and children, to be self-controlled, pure, working at home, kind, and submissive to their own husbands, that the word of God may not be reviled.
>
> (Titus 2:3–5, ESV)

The other major Abrahamic religions, Judaism and Islam, have similarly embraced both the submission of women and the fear of their inherently dangerous nature as major organising frameworks for the treatment of the female sex. As a result, penal codes in regions where these religions have dominated have also reflected these ideas.

Religious codes and practices have often subjected women's behaviour to special attention. Women were singled out as a significant object of punishment during the period of the Inquisition, which sought the extermination of heretics; additionally the charge of witchcraft was most often pursued against the female sex (Smith 1962:60). The dominant religions in the east have been equally discriminatory in their monitoring of women, with the possible exception of Buddhist teachings which professed equality between the sexes (Conze 2008). Misogynist and male-centred readings of Hindu scriptures and Islamic scholarly texts, however, have substantially influenced the penal code of much of the Asian continent and have, for centuries, denied full rights to women and severely limited their access to justice across that region of the world and in other areas where these religious teachings have prevailed (Conze 2008, Jones-Pauly 2011, Peters 2005, Sinha 2012). Confucianism has in a similar vein adopted a different set of rules for the female sex, embedded in patriarchal mores, which have restricted women and girls to domestic duties and an unflinching obedience to men (Gao 2003).

The colonisation of much of the world from the time of the Spanish conquistadors by predominantly Christian nations helped spread discriminatory attitudes towards women across the global south. Far from bringing more enlightened attitudes towards women in its wake and despite its claims to be a civilising and modernising force, imperialism imposed Christian perspectives and values onto the colonised nations which further reinforced extant chauvinistic and prejudicial attitudes towards the female sex. In India, for example, Sinha (2012) writes, the British governors, while they might have privately opposed the more barbaric practices involved in women's subjugation such as the practices of purdah, sati and the marriage of female children, remained generally silent on their attitudes to the privatised punishment meted out to women and girls and in public adopted a policy of non-intervention on matters of custom and tradition. It is suggested that there have been seismic shifts in the balance of power between the sexes and in women's access to justice. Before the writing of the Manusmriti, the traditional Hindu religious codebooks, women enjoyed equal status to men and Jones-Pauly (2011:xvii) argues that ancient Islam was in its early manifestations 'revolutionary in its gender relations for the time'; however, as we have seen here, over the ensuing centuries the balance of power clearly shifted in favour of the male sex.

Retributive principles and the undervaluing of the female sex

Retributive theories have dominated religious teachings on punishment. Retributive principles have considered punishment as a moral imperative requiring that a wrongful act be repaid by a punishment which 'fits' the crime and that the punishment should, by mirroring the crime, be seen to make recompense to the one who has been wronged. The most well-known of these strictures suggests 'an eye for an eye, a tooth for a tooth', a maxim which 'is deeply embedded in Judeo-Christian religion' (Newman 1978:190). Retributive theories also lie behind the granting of 'blood-money' as compensation to the families of murder victims, a practice still evident in a particular interpretation and application of Islamic law which is still prevalent in some countries. Retributive approaches to punishment claim a neutrality towards both the law-breaker and the victim with a focus instead on the crime committed, maintaining the principle that approved levels of punishment depend on the severity of the crime alone. In practice, however, designated punishments have not been proportionate in quality or kind. Retributive principles are wide open to discriminatory practices. They involve a measurement of the harm done to the victim which involves a consideration and calculation of the victim's worth and the court's ability to compensate for the damage experienced. Some types of victims have been considered more valuable than others, attracting a higher blood-price, while those considered of a lesser worth or value are compensated to a diminished extent. In some legislative codes, for example, the blood-price of any woman or of a non-Muslim male has been calculated to be half that granted for the loss of a Muslim man (Peters 2005:51).[1] Retributive punishment has been applied inequitably because society itself is riven with inequalities and as a consequence of patriarchal social ordering females have been denied even-handed treatment. Males have been awarded more status, with crimes committed against them considered more socially harmful. With the female sex afforded so little status in society, her possibility of gaining any sort of justice through the application of retributive principles was severely curtailed.

Whilst retributive practices were said to have been superseded by more liberal and enlightened thinkers in the eighteenth century (further discussed below), the 1970s witnessed a revival of retributive principles initially in the US (Howe 1994). The modern-day retributivists returned to these older principles in order, they argued, to remove what they perceived as discriminatory practices which had pervaded the workings of the criminal justice system. According to these liberal and progressive penologists, punishments in modern judicial systems had become too divorced from their link to the crime committed. Instead, judicial discretion had led to a disparity in sentencing and had become a source of inequality and discrimination in itself. The power to punish and detain, these writers argued, had been handed over to individual sentencers, parole boards and probation officers who in assessing individual risks were applying negative stereotypes to certain social groups or demanding acquiescence to a set of behaviours before parole could be considered (Hudson 2003:39–40). Female law-breakers, especially those who did not conform to social expectations, were considered as a particular risk, as doubly deviant and therefore punished for the crime of stepping outside their expected female role as well as for the crime itself (Heidensohn 1987). Locking punishment back into the crime committed, these writers argued, removed a process of decision-making which was informed by and tainted with social prejudice and thereby protected females from the invidious effects of sexual discrimination within systems of criminal justice.

The masculinism of modern punishment

The theories of punishment developed during the Enlightenment period were meant to break from the religious strictures and discriminatory attitudes of old. The philosophers of the Enlightenment period set out to replace outdated moralistic and retributive formulations of punishment with a rational model based on reasoned argument and humanitarian consideration as to its necessity, formulated in the late eighteenth and early nineteenth centuries most famously by Cesare Beccaria (1738–1794) and Jeremy Bentham (1748–1832). These 'modernisers' of the law and penal institutions made substantial inroads into the forging of new approaches to punishment in the emerging nation-states of their era. Punishment was subsequently regarded not as a moral prerogative or as a privilege of power but as a necessary evil which must be employed with care and which must be justified in all cases. Punishment was recognised as a harmful process which should be sparingly applied and which should always lead to a greater good. Consequently it was important that punishment be proportionate, moderate and state-sanctioned. Henceforth punishment was to be meted out only by those individuals who were empowered to do so by the state and was to be conducted in accordance with the law of that state. These penal reformers considered their approach to be driven by more humanitarian principles (Garland 2001). Their humanist and rights-based stance should have removed some of the arbitrary, privatised punishment meted out to women; however, their view of humanity was limited to the 'universal man' of law which omitted women from its range of vision (Naffine 1987:4).

Utilitarian principles were devised to account for the behaviour of the 'rational man', excluding women who were largely considered as irrational, childlike creatures, more driven by emotion than reason. Both Beccaria and Bentham claimed a more progressive view of women and their capabilities but did little to ensure that these were generally enshrined in their theories of the law and its practice. In his treatise *On Crimes and Punishments*, for example, Beccaria wrote that he considered women intelligent enough to be able to testify in court and to be considered as credible witnesses and he also included an attack on the power of the patriarch in family life; nevertheless he 'never speaks as to the place of women in his modern republic' (Messbarger 2002:7). At a time when the 'woman question' was beginning to emerge as a serious subject of debate, one of the most prominent social commentators failed to address women's relationship to punishment or to consider their unequal access to the protection of the law (Messbarger 2002). Bentham too is guilty of this neglect. While Bentham considered himself an advocate of women's political, legal and social rights who sympathised with the emerging demands for the extension of these rights to women, he considered that the time was not right to push forward on these feminist principles. He defended this stance by declaring that men were not ready to accept women as equals and that males were not mature enough to work with women in a mature and serious manner without considering them as sexual objects, or vulnerable beings first rather than as individuals with rights and mental capacities comparable to their own. Females who were brought before the courts as law-breakers therefore continued to face a double burden of discrimination. They were at one and the same time considered as fanciful and unthinking yet were tried and held to account by a system which was devised with only men's social positioning and freedom of action in its sight. This double burden placed the female sex in a particularly invidious position, set them up to fail dismally in obtaining justice within a flawed androcentric system and exposed women and girls to a multitude of harmful practices and painful experiences in the name of punishment. Yet utilitarian principles were supposed to outlaw punishment where this would do more harm, economically or socially, than not to punish.

Utilitarianism and formal equality

Utilitarian punishment regimes involved a shift to focus on the motivations of the potential law-breaker rather than to respond to the offence which they had committed. The law-breaker was considered as a rational actor making decisions on utilitarian principles, in order to maximise their individual pleasure and minimise their pain. The point of punishment was to add to the possible pains which might arise from any course of action which involved a decision which might harm another and in doing so, break the law. In addition the existence of punitive sanctions was to act as a constant reminder to the potential law-breaker that they would be held individually accountable for their decisions. In theory, women and men would be equally judged and equally punished. This line of thinking might have guided utilitarian theorists to consider the different personal paths which lie behind law-breaking and, as a consequence, might have addressed women's particular position in this respect, but this possible approach did not inform their deliberations. Their arguments, as those which preceded them, were based on what they considered to be a universal position and a particular view of the motivations which propelled all individuals into law-breaking. In this period equality was understood as ensuring sameness of treatment – a principle known as *formal equality*. As no person was to be held above the law, everyone was to be considered equally accountable and modern systems of law and punishment were to be enforced equally without regard to a person's social standing or stature. *Formal equality* was based on the Aristotelian ideal of fairness which proposed that rules should be applied consistently across the board without prejudice or discrimination.

In an apparent contradiction to the principles of formal equality, however, Bentham did propose different treatment for women who had stepped outside of the socially imposed moral boundaries of the time. His proposals for the building of a Sotimion (for adult women) and Nothotrophium (for children) are less well-known than the Panopticon with which he is most often associated. Bentham proposed and even drew up plans for institutions which would house unmarried pregnant women and illegitimate children, respectively. These establishments were partly protective, partly preventative but also places of containment. They were designed to provide accommodation and socially respectable occupations for women and children who had been excluded from 'decent' society, with the hope that they would be less likely to turn to crime as a consequence. Mirroring later visions of women-only provision for female law-breakers developed in the late twentieth century, Bentham's vision for the Sotimion benefited from feminine décor, incorporated social spaces and a coffee shop for women to meet and support each other and included flower and vegetable gardens as well as the opportunity to indulge in female-appropriate pastimes such as needlework, fruit preserving and ironing (Williford 1975:172–175).

Utilitarianism in an unequal world

Utilitarian principles of punishment rested on belief in a just and fair legal system which was impartial and applied equitably. Its proponents had no sense of women's double burden of punishment and how this affected the sentencing and punishment of the female sex. As we are now aware, women's pathways to crime often differ from those of men (Daly 1994). Women's law-breaking is often a reaction to their own marginalisation and control at the hands of men and comes about as a consequence of their lack of power and status. Their law-breaking also takes place within a discriminatory legal framework which restricts women's opportunity to access solutions which are allowed in law. Women, at the time of the so-called 'enlightenment', were damned by the law to the miseries of a life without social or economic power and without legal agency but were equally damned by a system set up to punish those who stepped outside the bounds of a system which suffocated their lives and denied them the opportunity to resist injustices which were ingrained into the very system itself. In treating men and women the same, these basic inequalities and discrimination with which the female sex battled daily were not considered as major contributing factors in their decision-making. With the exception of Bentham's architectural solutions for the care of 'fallen women' and children born outside of wedlock, utilitarian theories of punishment barely touched on the appalling position of women in society. The proponents of utilitarianism simply did not make the connection between women's subjugation, the social controls which so severely restricted the options available to women and girls and their law-breaking, and it was not until the last decades of the twentieth century that attention was turned to these issues.

As outlined earlier, the purpose of punishment under utilitarian principles was seen as being to build a better, more enlightened society in the course of which people would learn to desist from law-breaking, therefore leaving the populace as free of harm perpetrated by 'man' as could be achieved in reality. In the final analysis, the failure of utilitarianism to link theories of punishment to the particular conditions which face the female sex in law, in the practices of criminal justice and in society more generally meant that the principle that punishment should minimise harms and improve social conditions was far from achieved for the female sex. Neither did utilitarianist ideals make much impact on the position of women in society more generally. While feminists continued to petition for the rights of women to be respected and for women's full inclusion into the institutional frameworks of society, a feminist analysis of punishment was not forthcoming for another century and a half. The utilitarian perspective however did foster a concern to design and build a penal system which was humanitarian in its approach and in its practice. This paved the way for various reforms to the practice of punishment and for a fuller discussion as to the merits of sanctions such as incarceration which has still not abated today.

The reform movement and women's prisons

During the course of the development of utilitarian approaches, the imprisonment of women (and of children) did feature as a significant concern for some social reformers. The first of these, John Howard (1727–1790), was mainly concerned with the morality of women housed in penal institutions and called for women to be housed separately from 'the contaminating presence of lewd and rowdy males' (Dobash, Dobash and Gutteridge 1986:36). The Quaker Elizabeth Fry (1780–1845), who is well-known for her intervention in the area of women's imprisonment, was similarly exercised. Fry was particularly concerned with the terrible conditions in Newgate Prison and on convict ships, both of which she considered particularly unsuitable for women. She was initially driven by a belief that female prisoners could be successfully rehabilitated and that they were not, as many believed, beyond redemption. Fry advocated for women-only prisons staffed by female wardens (partly to reduce their exposure to assault and partly to provide positive female role models and a sympathetic ear), arguing that women had particular needs which could not be met in prisons which were designed for men. It was not until 1839, however, that the Prison Act made it unlawful for men and women to be imprisoned together (Camp 1974).

Driven by her particular ethical and moral principles, Fry instigated both educational and vocational training for women so that on release they could better support themselves and their families in the hope that this would deter them from future law-breaking. She considered women who had been imprisoned for prostitution as representing a special population which should be separated from the other female prisoners and subject to further moral and religious guidance (Pollock-Byrne 1990). With Fry's insistent campaigning, conditions for women prisoners were greatly improved and, as she predicted, recidivism rates for women dropped dramatically from around 35 to 4 per cent (Kilty 2014). Fry set up the Association for the Improvement of the Females at Newgate Prison, bringing female staff and volunteers into prison in order to guide female prisoners. She specified particular techniques which she believed were appropriate for dealing with women and emphasised the importance of prisoners voluntarily participating in 'their own transformation' (Dobash, Dobash and Gutteridge 1986:45). The prisoners were regulated by a system of rules which were based upon commonly held feminine ideals strictly forbidding swearing, playing cards, reading plays and novels, and the singing of 'immoral' songs; instead, women were expected to undertake typical domestic chores such as patchwork, needlework, spinning and knitting (Smith 1962, Dobash, Dobash and Gutteridge 1986). By 1825, however, Fry had moved away from her previous assertion that women could be reformed through their own voluntary efforts, and instead subjected women to a system of distinct punishment consisting of continuous, unremitting surveillance, strict discipline and hard labour (Dobash, Dobash and Gutteridge 1986: 57).

Fry was probably the earliest female campaigner to work around the imprisonment of women. Her approach was *sex-specific* in that it considered women and girls to have different needs than men and boys and that without recognition of these needs women would be damaged and brutalised. Fry also raised the radical notion that women in prison should be subjected to a different regime of treatment and proposed an approach which was attentive to differences between the sexes. Her *sex-specific* methods, initially at least, suggested that given care and attention to their difference and given access to sex-appropriate education, religious and moral instruction, women prisoners could begin to thrive. Fry's influence outside England was widespread, influencing prison regimes in Canada, the US, France, Denmark, Wales and Australia (Kilty 2005). Fry's arguments were shot through with the patriarchal and paternalistic attitudes of the period. They were certainly not revolutionary in tone; she did not advocate the abolition of prisons nor question the existence of punishment more widely, indeed her model for the 'treatment' of women in penal institutions gained remarkable results. Neither did her work question the place of women in society more widely. Fry's concern was to return female prisoners to respectability within society, to defer to their position and to better cope with their particular lot in life. As Fry tellingly proclaims, her wish was to teach women the 'habits of order, sobriety and industry which may render them docile and perceptible whilst in prison, and respectable when they leave it' (Biography Online 2017).

In effect the women's reformatories which Fry helped to establish, while they represented a radical departure from the form taken by masculinist penal establishments, succeeded in 'creating a set of feminised penal practices' (Rafter 1985:288) which continued to control working-class women's sexuality and to punish them for their response to poverty notwithstanding that this took place within facilities which were clean and less physically overbearing. Women's prisons were built on different design principles which acknowledged a collective spirit of women, designed as shared cottages rather than rows of identical and impersonal cells which separated one prisoner from another for long periods of time. Women's prisons were nonetheless still harsh and demeaning places with strictly enforced petty rules aiming to instil femininity and morality into their inmates. The building of women's prisons was instigated a little later in the US but there too *sex-specific* women's prisons were initially 'feminised' with reformers convinced of the view that women's innate morality and purity would be encouraged in spaces which were built around their feminine sensibilities (Pollock-Byrne 1990). The men and women who were driving these reforms were not advocates of women's political, social and economic rights, indeed some were very vocal in their opposition to extending rights to women; instead they were motivated by a view of women as in need of guidance and the feminine touch to bring them back into good order (Pollock-Byrne 1990). Women's prisons in the US were therefore set up as 'reformatories' which aimed to replicate family structures and responsibilities.

By the mid-twentieth century, however, these separate institutions for women gradually adopted more prison-like structures and regimes so that they came to resemble the maximum-security prisons which had been designed to incarcerate what were considered to be dangerous and violent men (Howe 1994:136).

Realist approaches to women's punishment

The first realist approaches to punishment were developed in Italy towards the end of the nineteenth century. They were developed as a critique of Beccaria's optimistic view that utilitarian approaches would lead to gradual improvements in society and that crime rates would drop as a result. Faced with rising crime and more punishment, theorists such as Enrico Ferri and Cesare Lombroso argued that society must be defended against the criminal. They considered that there were different 'criminal types', some of whom could be reformed through punishment but others who were criminal as a result of hereditary factors could not respond to punishment of any kind. The latter, they suggested, should be bred out of existence but the former might be persuaded out of crime through forms of treatment and rehabilitation. According to Ferri (1917), punishment on its own had no deterrent effect so incarceration was justified as a protective mechanism and as a means of giving society some respite from the offender. Rehabilitation or treatment was entered into as a secondary mechanism to protect society from an incarcerated individual's possible future law-breaking. The realist perspective opened the way to indeterminate sentences and also to consequentialist and reductionist strategies wherein someone who has not committed a crime but who might be considered at risk of law-breaking might be imprisoned for the future benefit of society. Lombroso's further development of the classification of individuals into 'criminal types' through the use of scientific method was part of this pre-crime risk assessment and led the positivist school to focus once again on the criminal propensities of individuals.

Lombroso and his research partner Ferrero famously considered female law-breakers to be particularly 'intense and perverse', 'more savage', morally deficient and 'less sensitive to pain' than their male counterparts (Lombroso and Ferrero 1895/2004). They considered all women as child-like, vengeful and prone to jealous rage, possessing an inferior intellect and an inability to control their passions. Consequently the born female criminal was 'doubly exceptional, first as a woman and then as a criminal'; they concluded that 'the criminal woman is a true monster' (Lombroso and Ferrero 1895/2004:183–185). However, Lombroso's insistence that most women law-breakers were not born criminal but came to law-breaking as a consequence of their social environment and lifestyle led him to argue that female law-breakers should not be incarcerated for their crimes as they were most likely to have been pushed into crime by social pressures (Rafter and Gibson 2004:20). In Lombroso's writing can be seen both a nod to the old ideas based in Christian scriptures which considered women as prone to lying, deceit and revenge but also the development of a different set of views of the female sex which have gained some popularity and which are shared by many feminist criminologists today: that women are not likely to be inherently prone to crime, that it is personal and social circumstances which push them into breaking the law and that they are more easily led away from law-breaking than are men. At the same time his views that women who break the law are worse than men who commit the same crimes, that they are doubly delinquent in transgressing feminine codes of conduct as well as the law of the land, and that women are particularly difficult to work with have also continued to dominate and impact on the way female law-breakers are perceived in mainstream criminology and criminal justice practice.

The rehabilitative turn

The rehabilitative ideals first espoused by utilitarians and later developed by realists dominated discourses around punishment well into the latter years of the twentieth century (Hudson 2003:153). The emergence of the social sciences and their impact on the study of crime led to the view that social and environmental factors play a large part in providing the circumstances in which individuals make their decision to break the law. While rehabilitative regimes were initially universally applied, the eventual classification of prisoners into different criminal types, along with the maturation of disciplines such as psychology and psychiatry, meant that different treatment regimes were eventually tailored to the category of prisoner they were intended to reform. During the 1960s a rehabilitative 'back to justice' movement, driven by a concern to ensure that punishment was applied with the clearest humanitarian principles to guide its severity and extent, began to make the case that rehabilitation should be tailored to the individual offender's needs rather than be generally applied depending on the type of crime committed (Carlen 1989, Matthews 1986, Rotman 1990). This approach was considered as protecting the rights of the individual law-breaker and ensuring that their personal, social and economic circumstances would be taken into account in their sentencing and subsequent treatment by the penal system. Rehabilitative principles acknowledge that while individuals do make their own choices, they do so in circumstances which are not of their choosing and which can severely limit their opportunities to act differently. This approach also recognises that the state, authorities and the powerful in society should bear some responsibility for creating those circumstances in which individuals' lives are constrained and therefore have the responsibility to provide some mechanism through which they can offer something back to the individual whose life has been made desperate and marginal. Consequently both parties offer something to the table: the law-breaker would devote their attention to changing their behaviour and the authorities would in turn offer them opportunities previously denied such as education, training or the mental training to allow the individual to adapt and change (Hudson 2003:62–66).

The significance of gender for practices of rehabilitative punishment

The rehabilitationist model opens up the field to a consideration of the gendered experiences of women and offers the beginnings of the position which has influenced many extant interpretations of *gender-specific justice* which are practised today. Firstly there is the humanitarian imperative which demands that society consider the law-breaker as an individual who retains their humanity and their human rights despite their law-breaking acts. The law-breaker is thus deserving of respect and dignity throughout the process of their punishment. Next this model requires that those who have the authority to sentence place the individual's acts within their social context and with the recognition that personal circumstances have a significant impact on the decision-making of individuals. Individuals should thereby be judged not simply by their actions but cognisant of the social pressures in which their acts take place and by which they are constrained. The idea of *gender-specific justice* adds the additional requirement for a full understanding of the specific pressures under which females are placed and suggests that we look beyond sex stereotypes based on the male/female binary to consider how women's lives are shaped by gendered social and cultural relations. The *gender-specific* approach also demands that women be considered in their totality, that to tackle the problems women face and to turn their lives around necessitates a consideration of the individual woman's entire experience, not just her law-breaking but the circumstances in which those law-breaking acts take place. It requires that her domestic situation, her lifestyle, her economic position, her capacity to act, her strengths, weaknesses, hopes and fears are all integral parts of her experience and that in effect a *holistic* approach is essential. The model also requires that women be approached with compassion and empathy but not to see the law-breaker as a victim so much as to consider her as exposed to economic, social and personal vulnerabilities (Corston 2007) which shift and alter throughout her life-course. Finally the model acknowledges women's agency and resilience, the power of women to change, to overcome adversity and to remodel their lives if given the opportunity and the right circumstances.

The new rehabilitation arguments have opened up the debate around punishment, its purpose and justification to a much wider interpretation. They set different approaches and goals to rehabilitation and have offered an optimistic assessment of what could be achieved in terms of behavioural change. However, these arguments have also been constrained by their essentially realist position. They have remained firmly within the punishment paradigm, looking to improve punishment, to rethink its purpose but in order that *punishment* would prove more effective in turning people to more 'law-abiding' lives. This more liberal reassessment, therefore, has still clung to the same 'technicist penology' which has hampered the ability to think more creatively and radically about the problem of crime. As Hudson explains, a technicist penology may include critical thinking, it can reveal the flaws in the current system, the harms which are created by punitive practices and can make important improvements to existing systems; however, in the final analysis:

> 'technicist' penology as opposed to the 'social analysis of penality' … simply aimed at helping those with the power to punish put their ideas into practice … administrative or technicist penology and criminology accept, rather than question, the aims of punishment espoused by the state. The problems they seek to resolve are second order questions such as what type of prison regime will serve the needs of reform, or public protection, or retribution; how prisons can be managed so as to minimise disorder and maximise security; what kind of non-custodial penalities will satisfy the penal aims of protection, retribution and rehabilitation.
>
> (Hudson 2003:10)

Hudson (2003: 63–64) recounts the many achievements of the new rehabilitation approach. It succeeded in raising the issue of prisoners' rights, in reducing levels of punitive response and the use of capital punishment and physical torture, in improving prisoners' access to education and training, in getting prisoners out of their cells for longer periods of time and in preparing prisoners for reintegration into the community. The state and penal authorities were held to account and forced to recognise their duty of care towards those who were imprisoned. Nevertheless, while some proponents of humanitarian principles in rehabilitation recognised that the harms of imprisonment often outweighed the advantages, they did not go down the abolitionist route.

Radical reactions

During the nineteenth century more radical writers and activists began to address punishment itself as a social harm and to argue for its complete eradication. Karl Marx, while writing little on crime and punishment directly, made it clear that he believed that legal and penal codes served to preserve an inherently unequal social order in which the interests of the propertied were defended at the expense of the poor and dispossessed (Taylor, Walton and Young 1973). While eschewing the idea that all instances of law-breaking are 'self-conscious acts of rebellion against an unjust authority' (Smith and Fried 1974 in Tunick 1992:48), radical writers inspired by Marxist theory have considered punishment nevertheless to be an inherently political practice:

> since it is the end-product of decisions to treat some social harms as deserving of penal sanctions and others as not – with little regard to the actual extent of social damage.
>
> (Smith and Fried 1974 quoted in Tunick 1992:48)

These radical thinkers raised some important issues. They inspired debates about the aims of punishment and questioned its very existence. They argued that penal systems do not exist as a means to reduce crime but serve more covert, disciplinary functions and they questioned the state's authority and competence to deliver justice. They failed as others had before them, however, to comment on the almost universal dispossession of the female sex, her particularly vulnerable position in society and man's almost complete exercise of power over the female body, concentrating instead on inequalities between the different economic classes which constitute society.

Subsequent Marxist analyses of punishment have mainly looked to explore ways in which the economy and punishment regimes are linked. In the labour market hypothesis suggested by Rusche and Kirchheimer (1939), for example, it was posited that punishment regimes are relaxed in times of labour shortage and made more punitive when labour is in plentiful supply. For these writers the purpose of punishment was to regulate the labour supply and to ensure that there was a steady supply of labourers for the land, for the military in times of war and especially to supply the newly emerging factories in a period of rapid industrialisation with a ready and willing workforce. They speculated that punishment was made particularly harsh in order that it was always worse than the alternatives on offer. This hypothesis was tested by others such as Box and Hale (1982) in the UK who made the important contribution that punishment is not always related to law-breaking and that it can serve other social, economic and political functions helping to maintain the status quo, to discipline the powerless and to keep them in a place where they best serve the interests of the powerful. As a consequence of their analysis and the decoupling of punishment from crime, many Marxists, neo-Marxists and anarchists have taken an abolitionist stance calling for the closure of prisons and a redrawing of laws on a more egalitarian basis. Some have questioned the existence of the entire criminal justice apparatus in capitalist society, speculating that punishment might not exist in post-capitalist social formations. As we shall see in later chapters, however, this call has been criticised by many writing from the perspective of the female sex who are so often victims of men's power and control but are equally unable to ensure that their victimisation is recognised or to obtain justice for the crimes committed against them. The labour theory of punishment also failed to account for fluctuations in the imprisonment of women and to acknowledge that women's role as providers of domestic labour was not incorporated in the analysis.

Where Marxist and feminist accounts have found more shared ground is in the adoption of the Marxist concepts of ideology and hegemony which seek to explain how certain ideas which may be against the interests of the majority can become so deeply entrenched in a society's values. The general acceptance and indeed popularity of the institution of punishment, the approval expressed for capital punishment, torture and other harsh authoritarian controls and punitive power during particular historical periods can only be understood with reference to these processes whereby the values of the ruling class are driven down throughout society and come to be accepted as the norm and as advantageous to the maintenance of social order. It is by using these concepts that societies' paradoxical position towards female law-breakers can best be understood as they can reveal ways in which the patriarchal and misogynistic attitudes which have held powerful men in their positions can become normalised throughout society.

Discipline and control

Foucault's thesis on the function of punishment as laid out in his important work *Discipline and Punish* (Foucault 1979) is similarly concerned with punishment as an expression of power. Foucault contends that the modern forms of punishment which emerged from the Enlightenment project are no less inhumane and damaging to their subjects than those which had previously prevailed. Modern penal systems, he argued, may appear more humane on the surface but are as implicated in the desire to control and discipline the aberrant body as pre-modern systems were designed to be. In a desire to 'correct' the wayward and the undisciplined, Foucault saw a reproduction of dominant forms of power and order and an attempt to produce the 'obedient body' rendered docile and moulded to society's expectations. Foucault's arguments reveal that the link between crime and punishment has been constructed in order to conceal the true functioning of power and to engineer belief systems which attain the status of universal truths. Foucault consequently considers power as less akin to an object, something which can be possessed, transferred or withheld by any particular class, but more as an extensive and pervasive process which institutionalises and normalises dominant beliefs or discourses which are necessary for the maintenance of extant structures of power. He demands that we look again at the key correctional institutions in society in order to unmask the ways in which they perpetuate these networks of power and 'truth'. It is as necessary, he argues, to closely examine and interrogate the welfare state, the schools, universities, psychiatric institutions, social, youth and community services and workplace practices, as it is to critique the more coercive arm of the state and its penal estate along with the criminal justice institutions of police, courts and probation which are more clearly concerned with the monitoring and surveillance of the social body.

Foucault and poststructuralist accounts more generally have highlighted the importance of discipline, power and control within the private sphere and the ways in which punishment 'crosses over institutional boundaries' (White and Perrone 1997:151) while previous histories of punishment and studies of social control concentrated almost exclusively on the public sphere. Notwithstanding the fact that Foucault makes few references to either women or gender in his work (Armstrong 2003), his account of the disciplinary power of social and penal institutions has inspired poststructuralist and feminist accounts which have used his insights to reveal the hidden mechanisms of power which trap women inside powerful discourses which shape, constrain and limit the female experience. This 'disciplinary power' acts as an external coercive force but also as a pervasive mechanism of monitoring and surveillance in such a way that dominant norms are eventually individually internalised. As a consequence individuals reproduce the normative frameworks which are essential for the powers embedded in modern society to be continually recreated and sustained. Individuals become invested in the reproduction of these discourses, in attaining standards of normality through which they can achieve recognition; failure to perform adequately in meeting society's expectations is to invite abuse, humiliation and personal attack. Punishment and disciplinary power are invidious, are dispersed throughout everyday life and are not restricted to the law-breaker but invade the entire social body. In addition, they have a role to play in sustaining social order and, as subsequent feminist analysis has suggested (Howe 1994), in upholding conventions of family and gender and in appropriating the female sex as the actors who are responsible for holding community and family together, discouraging law-breaking, controlling the impetuosity of youth and socialising the next generation. In this respect women's lives are more regulated outside the institutions of criminal justice and more often through systems of health, welfare, education and the family. The disciplining of women in the private sphere can thereby help to account for the significantly fewer numbers who currently come into contact with the criminal justice system and who are subsequently disciplined by correctional establishments when measured against the numbers of men who are processed through the same system.

Feminist incursions into criminology

Foucault's work has been significant in understanding the concept and extent of social control mechanisms, the ways through which they can reproduce an attachment to the norms and values of society as well as their role in suppressing tendencies to deviance and law-breaking (Hudson 2003). Cain (1990) has argued that criminology has social control at its very core. For much of its existence as an academic discipline, however, criminology has had little to say about the social control of the female sex and even less to contribute on the role of gender in shaping the experiences of both men and women. Criminology remained stubbornly blind to these key aspects of social ordering until the late 1970s when studies began to emerge, led by women, which took these issues into serious consideration. As we will see, this research, by women and about women, drew very different conclusions concerning the locus and impact of discipline, control and punishment throughout society. One of the key contributions which feminist research and writing was able to make was to use the concept of 'disciplinary control' to understand the victimisation of women by individual men, but which is normalised and sanctioned through patriarchal structures of power and control (Howe 1994:118). The female sex is subjected to punishment as an everyday experience of control and power over their bodies and the pain associated with the constant pressures of social censure and surveillance, of close monitoring and deprivation of freedoms, of feelings of worthlessness and of not quite measuring up to impossible standards, of being perceived as less than men and vulnerable to coercive and subtle controls whilst shouldering the burden of family life, caring responsibilities and making ends meet. For the female sex, formal systems of punishment add yet another layer of discipline and harmful practice onto lives which have already been largely broken by social pressures and sanctions (Carlen 1983).

The resurgence of discipline

The last quarter of the twentieth century witnessed a further shift in the disciplining of women. The data reveals that the imprisonment of women and girls appears to be on the increase in many regions of the world and additionally 'in some countries, at a faster pace than … for men' (Blanchette and Brown 2006:6).[2] This increase in the incarceration of women has been interpreted as evidence that women are becoming more troublesome and the emerging 'problem' has been largely understood in popular discourse and in mainstream criminological literature as a consequence of the increasing tendency for women to want to act just like men and therefore to behave as badly as men do. Within criminology this explanation has become known as 'the liberation hypothesis' following a theory developed by Freda Adler back in 1975 which has since been eagerly parroted by many to explain what they perceive as an increasing problem of females' involvement in criminal behaviour. With the exception of a very few studies and despite recent moral panics suggesting an exceptional and disturbing rise in the number of females breaking the law, however, the data demonstrates that women and girls are not 'catching up' with men in the field of criminality and that the ratio of males to females committing offences has remained remarkably stable for a long period of time (Blanchette and Brown 2006). So what explains the increased numbers of women and girls brought to the attention of the criminal justice system?

The increased willingness to arrest and charge women, and ultimately lock them up in prisons, can be attributed to a combination of social reactions which have played out concurrently and had significant effects within the criminal justice system. The first of significance, highlighted by Lahey (1985) and termed 'equality with a vengeance' or 'vengeful equity', suggests that criminal justice personnel have increasingly adopted the attitude that if women want to behave like men then they will be treated like men and without sympathy or favour. Whilst it was once believed that the criminal justice system was soft on females and extended leniency towards their misdemeanours (Pollak 1950), a growing body of evidence shows that, when compared with males who have committed similar acts, women and girls may actually be sentenced more harshly (MacDonald and Chesney-Lind 2001) and for longer periods (Belknap 1996), especially when they deviate from the feminine ideal (Steffensmeier and Demuth 2001). The second is that this has coincided with a general rise in punitive sentencing which has caught more females within its net. The subjective perception that females are becoming more liberated and troublesome therefore, is rather more a reason that there has been an increased criminalisation of women than any objective changes in the reality of their propensity to offend (Steffensmeier, Kramer and Striefel 1993). It is important to acknowledge that the brunt of this increase in criminalisation has fallen on particular sections of the female population. The data reveals that the increase in the number of females who have come into contact with the criminal justice system is not uniform across all social groups. Women of colour, indigenous women, women from certain religious and cultural minorities – and, in the West, foreign national women – are incarcerated in greater numbers than white women (Kalunta-Crumpton 2010). This trend has been explained as a consequence of the war on drugs which has driven many domestic and some foreign policy interventions in the US since the 1980s and which began to make its mark on the numbers in prison in that country from the 1990s onwards. The policies which were implemented in this 'war' have been disproportionately implemented within racialised communities within the US and some of the poorest and most vulnerable residents of these targeted neighbourhoods have fallen under the widening net of crime control as a result. The war on drugs, announced first in the US, has been exported to other regions of the globe and affected national policies outside the US' legislative jurisdiction. So while rates of imprisonment for women remain low, they have been increasing noticeably in many countries and the rise in numbers of females convicted and charged has meant that systems of criminal justice have become more significant to those in criminology who are interested in the experiences of women and girls.

Notes

1 The reintroduction of Sharia law in many countries across the Middle East and Africa in the last half of the twentieth century has been considered as a consequence of the rejection of modernism and the advance of secularist ideas but for many it symbolised and codified a rejection of imperialist domination and the 'westernisation' of society (Peters 2005). Where Sharia codes of law and punishment have been reconstituted, however, this has had a significant impact on women's legal

standing, raising concerns for feminists and human rights advocates alike (Salime 2011).

2 Blanchette and Brown's evidence demonstrates that this is the case in the US, Australia and the UK.

References

Adler, F. (1975) *Sisters in Crime: The Rise of the New Female Criminal*. New York: McGraw Hill.

Armstrong, A. (2003) 'Foucault and feminism', *Internet Encyclopedia of Philosophy*, https://philpapers.org/rec/ARMFAF [Accessed 12 July 2016].

Belknap, J. (1996) *The Invisible Woman: Gender, Crime, and Justice*. Belmont, CA: Wadsworth.

Biography Online (2017) 'Elizabeth Fry biography', www.biographyonline.net/humanitarian/elizabeth-fry.html [Accessed 22 March 2017].

Blanchette, K. and Brown, S.L. (2006) *The Assessment and Treatment of Women Offenders: An Integrative Perspective*. Chichester, UK: John Wiley.

Box, S. and Hale, C. (1982) 'Economic crisis and the rising prisoner population in England and Wales', *Crime and Social Justice*, 17: 20–34.

Cain, M. (1990) 'Towards transgression: new directions in feminist criminology', *International Journal of the Sociology of Law*, 18(1): 1–18.

Camp, J. (1974) *Holloway Prison: The Place and the People*. Newton Abbot, UK: David and Charles.

Carlen, P. (1983) *Women's Imprisonment: A Study in Social Control*. London: Routledge and Kegan Paul.

Carlen, P. (1989) 'Crime, inequality and sentencing', in Carlen, P. and Cook, D. (eds), *Paying for Crime*. Milton Keynes: Open University Press, pp. 8–28.

Carrington, K. (2015) *Feminism and Global Justice: New Directions in Critical Criminology*. London: Routledge.

Conze, E. (2008) *Buddhism: A Short History*. London: One World Publications.

Corston, J. (2007) *Women with Particular Vulnerabilities in the Criminal Justice System*. London: Home Office.

Daly, K. (1994) *Gender, Crime, and Punishment*. New Haven, CT: Yale University Press.

Dobash, R.P., Dobash, R.E. and Gutteridge, S. (1986) *The Imprisonment of Women*. London: Wiley Blackwell.

Ferri, E. (1917) *Criminal Sociology*. Translated by J.I. Kelly and J. Lisle. Boston, MA: Little, Brown and Company.

Foucault, M. (1979) *Discipline and Punish: The Birth of the Prison*. London: Vintage Books.

Gao, X. (2003) 'Women existing for men: Confucianism and social injustice against women in China', *Race, Gender & Class*, 10(3): 114–125.

Garland, D. (2001) *The Culture of Control: Crime and Social Order in Contemporary Society*. Chicago, IL: University of Chicago Press.

Heidensohn, F. (1987) *Women and Crime: Questions for Criminology*. Milton Keynes: Open University Press.

Howe, A. (1994) *Punish and Critique: Towards a Feminist Analysis of Penality*. London: Routledge.

Hudson, B. (2003) *Understanding Justice: An Introduction to Ideas, Perspectives and Controversies in Modern Penal Theory.* Buckingham: Open University Press.

Jones-Pauly, C. (2011) *Women under Islam: Gender, Justice and the Politics of Islamic Law.* New York: Palgrave Macmillan.

Kalunta-Crumpton, A. (ed) (2010) *Race, Crime and the Criminal Justice System: International Perspectives.* London: Palgrave Macmillan.

Kilty, J.M. (2005) *The Life and History of Elizabeth Fry.* New York: Sage.

Kilty, J.M. (2014) *Within the Confines: Women and the Law in Canada.* Toronto: Canadian Scholars Press.

Lahey, K. (1985) 'Until women themselves have told all they have to tell', *Osgoode Hall Law Journal*, 23(3): 519–541.

Lombroso, C. and Ferrero, G. (1895/2004) *The Female Offender.* New York: Appleton and Company.

MacDonald, J.M. and Chesney-Lind, M. (2001) 'Gender bias and juvenile justice revisited: longitudinal analysis', *Crime and Delinquency*, 47(2): 173–195.

Matthews, R. (1986) *Confronting Crime.* London: Sage.

Messbarger, R. (2002) *The Century of Women: Representations of Women in Eighteenth-century Italian Public Discourse.* Toronto: University of Toronto Press.

Naffine, N. (1987) *Female Crime: The Construction of Women in Criminology.* Boston, MA: Allen and Unwin.

Newman, G.R. (1978) *The Punishment Response.* Piscataway, NJ: Transaction.

Peters, R. (2005) *Crime and Punishment in Islamic Law: Theory and Practice from the Sixteenth to the Twenty-first Century.* Cambridge: Cambridge University Press.

Pollak, O. (1950) *The Criminality of Women.* Philadelphia: University of Pennsylvania Press.

Pollock-Byrne, J. (1990) *Women, Prison and Crime.* Pacific Grove, CA: Brooks/Cole.

Rafter, N.H. (1985) *Partial Justice: Women in State Prisons, 1800–1935.* Boston, MA: Northeastern University Press.

Rafter, N.H. and Gibson, M. (2004) *Criminal Woman, the Prostitute, and the Normal Woman, by Cesare Lombroso and Guglielmo Ferrero.* Durham, NC: Duke University Press.

Rotman, E. (1990) *Beyond Punishment: A New View of the Rehabilitation of Criminal Offenders.* Westport, CT: Greenwood.

Rusche, G. and Kirchheimer, O. (1939) *Punishment and Social Structure.* New York: Russell and Russell.

Salime, Z. (2011) *Social Movements, Protest and Contention: Between Feminism and Islam. Human Rights and Sharia Law in Morocco.* Minneapolis: University of Minnesota Press.

Sinha, C. (2012) *Debating Patriarchy: The Hindu Code Bill Controversy in India (1941–1956).* Oxford: Oxford Scholarship Online.

Smith, A. (1962) *Women in Prison: A Study in Penal Methods.* London: Stevens and Sons.

Steffensmeier, D. and Demuth, S. (2001) 'Ethnicity and judges' sentencing decisions: Hispanic–Black–White comparisons', *Criminology*, 39(1): 145–178.

Steffensmeier, D., Kramer, J. and Striefel, J. (1993) 'Gender and imprisonment decisions', *Criminology*, 31(3): 411–446.

Taylor, I., Walton, P. and Young, J. (1973) *The New Criminology: For a Social Theory of Deviance.* London: Routledge.

Tunick, M. (1992) *Punishment: Theory and Practice.* Berkeley: University of California Press.

White, R. and Perrone, S. (1997) *Crime and Social Control: An Introduction.* Melbourne: Oxford University Press.

Williford, M. (1975) 'Bentham on the rights of women', *Journal of the History of Ideas*, 36(1): 167–176.

Chapter 2

From sex-specific to gender-responsive justice

Opening up punishment to a feminist lens

As we can see from the discussion of theories of punishment introduced in Chapter 1, the ideas which have enabled societies to justify, legislate and regulate different punishment regimes have been assumed to be gender-neutral. Women's experiences remained largely un-noted with few references to women and only fleeting acknowledgement that women's position in relationship to regimes of punishment might be considered separately or as in any way differing from that of men. Even when critical criminology entered the field, 'there seems to have been a reluctance to conceive of punishments as being gender-specific' (Carlen 1983:3) with major critical offerings on the subject barely scraping the surface in this respect. Modern classics such as Garland's *Punishment and Society* written as late as 1990, at a time when feminist criminology had made some serious inroads into critical readings of the discipline, remained stubbornly gender-blind and seemingly unconvinced by the pleas of feminists within criminology to consider the position of women and to learn from the inclusion of feminist insights into theory-making. As a consequence discussions around justice for women and what it might look like are still very much in their infancy. Notwithstanding this late arrival on the scene, feminist critiques of penal regimes have had notable success in bringing the world's attention to a number of critical issues – one of these is the call for the building of a justice system which is attentive to women's needs and which is built on an awareness of the different needs of women and girls.

Before we turn to a consideration of the contribution which women's voices have made in this area, however, it is important to reflect on the problems which an androcentric viewpoint of justice has left women to struggle with. These issues are not just pertinent to women in the West, although many have been revealed by writers working in the Anglophone world, but their salience would seem to cross continental barriers. Whether the issues which feminism has introduced into the discipline are interpreted in similar ways in different cultural contexts is a question which this publication cannot answer; however, as we will see in later chapters, numerous national bodies and transnational organisations have recognised their relevance and have put in place strategies to help to counter discriminatory attitudes in criminal justice in different regions of the world, for these are indeed issues of global concern.

Saints and sinners: the stereotyping of women in the criminal justice system

The female sex has found it difficult to obtain equality within formal systems of criminal justice across the ages for many different reasons. The legislators, policy-makers, social workers and psychologists who legislate, classify, advise, rehabilitate and treat women who have come to the attention of the authorities for any reason are working with a script which has been written around a system of knowledge which is profoundly male-centred and which little understands women's needs (Hudson 1997). A number of particularly damaging stereotypes have endured which have been shown to have significantly affected women's access to formal justice over the ages. These stereotypes are baseless and mutually contradictory yet they remain deeply entrenched into the fabric of society. They are institutionalised into family, school, neighbourhoods, the media, national and local state authorities. They taint contact at all levels of the criminal justice system, where women and girls, whether entering the criminal justice system as victims or law-breakers, are subjected to the same stereotypes and discriminatory attitudes within police stations, lawyers' offices, courts, probation offices and prisons.

The deceitful woman

Women have been traditionally cast as treacherous and untrustworthy creatures. Within Christianity the female sex has been painted as the purveyor of original sin with Eve (and therefore womankind) painted as the original transgressor. Indeed, according to biblical tradition, the first punishment was justified as a necessary consequence of Eve's willingness to break God's injunction not to eat the forbidden fruit. In addition, however, Eve's very creation from the bent rib of man singled out the female of the species as defective, 'in contrary direction to man' and thereafter as naturally inclined 'to lies, deceit and concealment' (Newman 1978:88). This view of the female as mendacious and as an unreliable witness can also be seen outside the realms of the Christian world. In classical Sharia law, for example, some rules of evidence in criminal proceedings have stated that the testimony of women should not be considered as equal to that of the man, requiring two or more women to give evidence where one man's statement would be sufficient (Newman 1978:177). This evidential standard was also found within Christian Europe as late as the eighteenth century (Williford 1975:175).

Throughout the ages women's testimonies have been less likely to be believed and both women and girls have often been painted as the deceiver or false accuser. This belief in the duplicitous nature of the female sex was famously incorporated into the work of Otto Pollak in his influential study *The Criminality of Women* written in 1950 and can be traced through to the charge of false accusation often meted out to female victims of rape and/or sexual assault today. It is linked to the idea of the *vengeful woman*, who will falsely accuse in order to seek revenge for those who have slighted or harmed her. The refusal to believe the testimony of females is especially damaging when women report victimisation at the hands of intimate partners and in domestic settings where no other witnesses are available. It is all too often reported that the hierarchy of credibility (Becker 1967) still works in men's favour and that men's refutations and viewpoints are still given more credence than those of women and girls.[1]

The gentle woman

Another much-observed trope used against women is the portrayal of women as the 'gentle sex', less prone to violent outbursts or loud or raucous behaviour. The association of femininity with a quiet, softly spoken and placid demeanour has worked to deny women the use of their voice and their agency. During the Middle Ages and up to the eighteenth century in Britain and the US, women could be legally admonished for speaking out. 'Scolds' (who were almost invariably women) were subject to the punishment of the ducking stool to extinguish their fiery tongue or forced to wear painful, sometimes spiked, iron cages around their head and mouth as they were dragged around town (Newman 1978:97–98). Women could be classed as 'scolds' for their behaviour in private as well as public and therefore had to 'watch their tongue' and limit their criticisms of others, especially men, at all times. The condemnation of the outspoken woman can be linked to the view that women should be subordinate at all times to their 'lord and master' and also to the injunction that women should be seen to be respectable and to maintain the honour of their family, not only through their actions but also by their words. Women were expected to hold their opinions privately, to play their part in the background and not to seek to be visible, to step into the foreground or to air views which might be thought unpopular or challenging in any way (Peters 2005:63). The arena for argument and debate was considered distinctly masculine, as a natural arena for the thinking, rational male but unsuitable for the gentle, submissive female. It has been particularly difficult therefore for women to ensure that their accounts are heard in any trial situation; if they speak out they may be considered pushy and aggressive – traits which may not endear them to judges and juries – whereas to play to the usual stereotype of the quiet and uncomplaining female risks remaining unheard and misunderstood. In addition, to play the compliant and malleable female bears the risk of being considered as without agency and open to the accusation of being led by a more powerful protagonist into the commission of crimes as a joint enterprise. Women can consequently be implicated in the crimes committed by men close to them even when they do not play an active part. Women are therefore controlled and limited by social expectations at every turn – they are damned if they do speak out and can be equally damned if they do not.

When generally held stereotypes of femininity are challenged more widely this can also raise significant problems for the women entering the criminal justice system. The discovery of the female offender in the 1970s, for example, had serious consequences for the policing of women and girls. The last decades of the twentieth century witnessed an unprecedented number of women and girls being brought to the attention of the criminal justice system in many countries in the West with greater numbers both sentenced and imprisoned.[2] In the US these 'increases in girls' arrests [...] dramatically outstripped those of boys for most of the last decade' of that century, with violent and 'non-traditional' (sex-stereotyped) offences showing the greatest increases (Chesney-Lind and Okamoto 2001:2). The arrest statistics were greeted with dismay and some considerable concern as they challenged the 'gentle woman' stereotype. National policy-makers and the media bemoaned the rise of the 'ladette', young women whose growing financial and social independence allowed them to behave as young men have always done, being seen out in public spaces and indulging in heavy drinking and raucous behaviour. There was considerable moral panic raised too over the emergence of the 'gang girl', no longer hanging on the coat-tails of the young gang-involved male but forging her own way and forming her own gang independently of male influence (Chesney-Lind 1995). Popular explanations for the increase in women's sentencing and imprisonment blamed the popularity of feminism and its success in transforming the expectations of a generation of young women so that they had become seekers after male pleasures (Walter 1999:8–9). However, as many feminist criminologists argued, the increase in arrests and sentencing was more a function of a change in police behaviour, an increase in surveillance and regulation of young women and an increasing willingness on the part of the courts to sentence women more severely in order to signal to others that the bad behaviour of women and 'gender-bending' would not be tolerated (Chesney-Lind and Okamoto 2001).

The vulnerable woman

Women have been construed as weak and vulnerable creatures in need of protection – and that protection has almost always been considered as appropriately delivered by a suitable male preferably related by either kinship or marriage. Such 'protection' is a source of structural and personal vulnerability for both women and girls. Indeed it is in the 'protective custody' of the family that the majority of abuse and the coercive control of females takes place. In the absence of restraints imposed by family, however, the state, working through its systems of criminal justice and social care, has been all too willing to step in to take on this role. The control of the female sex by the male is often justified in the benign term of 'chivalry', a term which conveys a courteous, considerate and responsive attitude towards the needs of women but which is in reality more often a cover for further restricting women's rights, for overbearing restriction and the removal of women's agency. It is closely connected to a construction of masculinity as encompassing the ideals of bravery, valour and physical ability, suggesting of course that there is an absence of these qualities to be found within the female sex. The counterpart to the chivalrous man is the 'honourable' woman, for it is the honour and respectability of the female sex which the chivalrous male (the knight in shining armour) is most often intervening to protect.

It has been suggested many times that chivalry works in women's favour and could even account for their lower numbers in arrest data, in crime statistics – as victims are said to be reticent to report the law-breaking of women – and in sentencing and imprisonment as courts are less likely to find women guilty. It is suggested therefore that women are 'getting away with murder' (sometimes literally) (Adler 1975, Pollak 1950, Steffensmeier 1980). These claims have been tested and retested many times with contradictory results, demonstrating the complexity of the issues involved (Pollock-Byrne 1990:27). Research has also revealed that where differential judgements were indeed being applied to females these did not always benefit women and girls; on the contrary, those who bucked feminine stereotypes could be judged very differently to those who appeared more wedded to hegemonic feminine ideals (Farrington and Morris 1983). Similarly, research on young female juveniles has revealed that they are much more likely to be placed into institutional care than their male counterparts and that they are taken away from their families for very different reasons, many of which are not related to law-breaking but to the breaking of moral codes, especially around sexual behaviour where girls are expected to maintain more control than boys. Girls have been institutionalised for behaviour which was considered to be aggressive or risky when engaged in by girls but which was tolerated and accepted as a normal part of growing up when carried out by boys. As Chesney-Lind's research shows, 'incorrigibility', refusal to submit to parental controls or running away from home, all classed as 'status offences' in the US and Canada, have been dealt with severely by the courts in those countries in order to bring young females under some form of control (Chesney-Lind 1982). Research has also shown that women are more likely to be taken into protective custody for psychiatric assessment or treatment as a consequence of what is perceived to be poor behaviour.

The belief that women are vulnerable and in need of protection has led to some instances of *sex-specific* treatment regarding allowable punishments. In some regions where Islamic law is practised, women have been spared banishment as a consequence of the stricture that women are not permitted to live outside of their family without a male relative; in other regions, and for the same reasons, a close male relative must be banished alongside the woman in order to preserve her honour (Peters 2005:34). In Medieval Europe the manner of death inflicted by the courts when giving out a death penalty was gendered. It has been argued that the methods used on women, typically stoning, being buried alive and being burned at the stake, inflicted more pain than the methods used for the execution of men, demonstrating 'a will to punish female criminals in a harsher way' (Ekholst 2014:216). Others have suggested that the methods used for females were designed to destroy the woman's body, reflecting a reluctance to place women's bodies on display as hanging or breaking on the wheel would have done and a requirement to preserve the honour of the woman's body even in death (Ekholst 2014:217). In the same vein, in some areas utilising Islamic law women are whipped while seated rather than standing and do not have to remove their clothes (Peters 2005:35) and when being stoned women may be buried in the earth up to their waists possibly also to protect some part of their modesty (Peters 2005:37). In one particularly repulsive practice, women who failed to protect their honour sufficiently might in some areas have their vulva branded, giving them permanent stigmata which would advertise their 'dishonourable nature', inviting future condemnation and censure and acting as an invitation to males that they could abjure from chivalrous behaviour towards such an obviously tainted female (Peters 2005:101).

Women's imagined 'weakness' has also singled them out for special treatment in sentencing and punishment, but again the examples are few and far between. Some Islamic legal codes, for example, did not allow women to be charged with banditry as this charge rested on the assailants being possessed with superior strength to their victims so that the latter were unable to escape and this was felt to be beyond the physical capabilities of the female sex (Peters 2005:57). Additionally female apostates were spared execution as women were not considered as meeting the definition of 'enemy combatants' and therefore could not be considered as justly killed in war, holy or otherwise (Peters 2005:65). Where states which abided by Islamic law were colonised and subjected to 'modernisation' of their legislative frameworks by their mainly Christian invaders, many corporal punishments for women were withdrawn. Unfortunately the death sentences for women were instead commuted into imprisonment, which delivers its own particular set of harms and would normally be reserved for the most serious crimes. Similarly, in the current period there are examples of 'up-tariffing' where women are subjected to more serious sentences which are imposed in order to ensure that they are subject to ongoing care and protection by the state (Holdsworth and Hucklesby 2014).

Disciplinary regimes inside the carceral net: by women, for women

As we have seen in Chapter 1, the first sustained challenge to penal practices involving women was delivered by the early prison reformers who were driven by a desire to see improved conditions for incarcerated women. These reformers were motivated more by moral than political sensibilities and whilst the public reformatories for women which they built were cleaner and superficially more hospitable than the prisons in which women were formerly incarcerated, they could hardly be regarded as model institutions. In addition these middle-class reformers hardly understood the realities of life for the poor and desperate women who were likely to be placed into custody and so still subjected working-class women to impossible behavioural standards (Rafter 1985). While few women were incarcerated at this time and female prisoners were rarely perceived as a danger to society, women who broke the law were still considered a moral pollutant and expected to conform to particular standards of feminine behaviour before they could be successfully released into society. Failure to conform could result in harsh penalties, isolation and even the refusal of parole. These public reformatories which were run through the criminal justice arm of the state had their private counterparts, many of which were set up and run by religious organisations. These latter were not institutions in which women were sentenced to remain by the courts, but were extra-judicial institutional settings in which organisations supposedly concerned with the moral and physical welfare of vulnerable females might place women or girls in protective custody 'for their own good'. They include the notorious Magdalene laundries run by Christian nuns and 'established by several religious orders over 150 years in 67 countries' (Romero 2014) as well as asylums set up to provide care for those who were considered 'feeble-minded' but into which women could be committed for the 'sin' of having a child outside of marriage or enjoying extramarital sex (Cohen 2016). They were reformatories where 'fallen' women were kept to a strict regime of prayer and penitence. As Romero powerfully relates of her own 'enslavement' within a Magdalene laundry in Adelaide, Australia in 1967:

> All were organized around a single schedule, a template built on a hierarchy of power-work-silence-prayer – and an idea of cleansing us of our rotten sin – for the after-life. Like all enslavement and forced labor – this was a mechanism to break the spirit and inculcate set beliefs. But even more pernicious – it was based on the belief that the church was saving the community at large from the infection of vulnerable girls. This was the idea that fallen (a term they used for us) meant tainted=contagious.
>
> (Ruggles 1983:59)

These institutions were strictly run and seriously damaging to the women and girls forced to reside within them. They were deeply implicated in the control of women and girls both inside and outside of their walls. Although staffed by women these were not designed to provide caring, supportive environments in which women could thrive. They were female-only and *sex-specific* in their outlook admitting only female inmates and with female staff, but they could not be said to be 'feminised' or 'women-friendly'. Instead they were ordered through dominant masculinist perspectives and the treatment of their inmates was organised through religious codes which cast the residents, who were often unmarried mothers, as sinners and included a set of punitive practices which were retributive in principle, subjecting their inmates to hard labour and disciplining every aspect of their existence in order that they should pay for their transgressions. These institutions were far from rehabilitative in their approach. By the beginning of the twentieth century, at least in the US, women's prisons too had lost touch with the reformers' demands that institutions for women should be run on a different set of assumptions, that women should be treated differently to men and that women would respond more readily to kindness and sympathy than to harsh disciplinary regimes. One aspect of the early reforms did remain intact and this was that women's prisons should retain an emphasis on training women in domestic skills. As a result the physical design of the prisons based on domestic houses rather than cells remained but at the same time their female governors and staff absorbed the dominant discourses of imprisonment and reintroduced a set of masculinist ideas and values which maintained that the purpose of prison institutions was to remove freedoms, to demand conformity and to instil fear into the hearts of the inmates such that they would never wish to return (Freedman 1981, Rafter 1985).

Women's experiences and the pains of imprisonment

Once inside the prison gates women's experiences differed from those of men, although this too was not recognised until the entry of women into criminology departments in the 1970s meant that women's imprisonment was studied as a subject in its own right (Pollock-Byrne 1990). While women 'on the inside' bear the same injustices as men their imprisonment, as women, adds further to the pains which they suffer. The additional burdens faced by incarcerated females are multiple and varied. They may be related to the woman's family responsibilities: many imprisoned women are mothers and must endure the pain of separation from their children. Women in prison are often the main carers of their children and cannot rely on the father to take on these duties. Those with sole responsibility for their children's upbringing will have the added pain of knowing that their children will probably be placed in institutional care or allocated temporary foster families for the duration of their prison sentence. Women have different physical needs which are often not adequately met whilst they are incarcerated; there are added indignities in using public toileting facilities especially during menstruation or of negotiating pregnancy and birth while incarcerated. Their pain may be related to the injustice of women's double penalty and being locked out of society for minor infractions and misdemeanours which could be better addressed in the community. It could be that the imprisoned female body is particularly vulnerable to sexual voyeurism and assault within a place where there is no escape and moreover that strip-searching subjects the female body to a particular form of gendered violation. Or it could be that most women cannot or do not want to fit into the standardised ideal of 'woman' which is imposed upon them by petty rules and regulations which limit their self-expression and which denies them the power to be different. In addition it is still too often the case that women's opportunities for training and education are further limited by sex-stereotypes which deny them the opportunity to learn the skills which will help them to survive a hostile economic environment and to take care of themselves and their families once released. In addition, as we will see, women are likely to enter prison with physical, psychological, trauma-induced and substance abuse issues which have gone untreated in the past and are rarely addressed when they are inside. Or it is likely to be a combination or indeed all of these factors together which make the experience of incarceration so unbearable for female inmates.

Prison authorities have failed to understand the additional pressures which their regimes place on women and it is only in the last few decades that these issues have begun to be raised as a point of serious concern. Incarcerated females have been subjected to multiple disciplinary processes running parallel within the prison walls and as White relates, these have culminated in particularly acute forms of control in which women have been micro-managed and even 'disciplined for minor infractions like sitting in a chair sideways during a meal, coming to breakfast with their hair in pin curls, expressing negativity, and talking in an angry tone of voice' (White 2012:285). These *sex-specific* disciplinary regimes are additional to the usual disciplinary process to which men are also subjected. In addition both public and privately run custodial institutions and asylums serve a useful economic purpose, supplying a market in cheap domestic and industrial labour (Rafter 1985). In the case of incarcerated women their training was designed to skill them not only for the labour market but also for the domestic and reproductive functions assigned to their sex. The 'reforming process' for females was therefore particularly holistic in its vision and purpose to create functioning women out of a group which was considered as dysfunctional and disordered. Men's prisons did not concern themselves with the total reform of their inmates to the same degree. Missing from the male experience were these significant elements of gendered social control; men did not face incarceration for sexual misconduct and within prisons were not subject to the same crushing weight of moral responsibility, nor to the same severity of punishment for minor infringements of petty rules. Men have enjoyed greater freedoms both inside and outside the penal institution while women, by contrast, have had to endure significant levels of mental and physical humiliation and bodily mortification within the prison institution and have been inculcated with an enduring burden of shame and guilt which they have had to bear far beyond the prison walls.

Introducing gender-sensitive practices into prisons

The first reformers of the prison estate were concerned with the creation of *sex-specific* institutions, separating women from men and designing institutions which catered for the special needs of women, as they were understood at that time. The intervention of females into criminology and criminal justice practice in the latter part of the twentieth century, however, introduced a more sophisticated and nuanced analysis to the problem. The early reformers were liberal reformists, concerned with improving the experiences of women as a necessary and social good and in raising the issue of women's right to fair and decent consideration of their particular needs. They were driven by compassion towards women, and their children, but their reforming zeal was limited to a liberal reformist vision which did not extend to more radical critiques of the structures of power in society which so disadvantaged the female sex. These reformers were driven by a set of moral values which could not encompass a critique of the masculinist frameworks of knowledge and understanding which these forms of morality had been built around. Furthermore, these reformers did not identify as feminists but as intelligent and compassionate women who wanted to right certain wrongs which were routinely done to the female sex. Second-wave feminism, however, was built around a more radical critique of patriarchy and of a set of masculinist assumptions pertaining to women and their role in society.

Second-wave feminism was not just concerned with the granting of equal rights to women, but was also concerned to unpack the problem of gender and its impact on social relations. This wave of feminism was built on a more radical social critique, using the work of feminists such as Simone de Beauvoir, bell hooks and Susan Brownmiller; it fostered a movement which demanded the liberation of women and the dismantling of the patriarchal social structures which kept all women in a state of oppression. It was their use of the concept of patriarchal power which allowed feminists to identify the specific and gendered ways in which women are victimised by the structures of society and by individual men, the gendered nature of social institutions which advantage men and their conceptual frameworks. They also introduced a materialist basis for women's 'ways of knowing' which differ from male knowledge and which are based on women's shared experiences of oppression rather than on the practices of privilege which are common to the experiences of both men and boys. This more radical lens posited that existing sets of social relations and social institutions had been developed by men, for men and that it was impossible to fit women into masculinist frameworks which represented examples of male hegemony and control over women's minds and bodies (Smart 1989). Second-wave feminism therefore advocated the removal of male sources of power and their replacement by women-centred organisational structures which were informed by women's knowledge and experiences. Second-wave feminists proposed the adoption of a different set of logics and values based in women's unique perspective which would challenge the oppressive practices of men, place women at the centre of knowledge production, and give priority to the female voice which had been subjugated for so long, the raising of women's consciousness and the sharing of ideas between women so that new organisational practices could be developed and implemented. Their early frameworks for action were women-centred and argued that women should act together, free from male interference in order that they could re-evaluate the role of women and discover sources of power, strength and connectivity which resided in the feminine body and psyche.

Once the values and methods of second-wave feminism were brought to the attention of criminology they began to make an impact on the ways in which this more critical section of the discipline considered and operationalised its key concepts. Women were introduced to the discipline as victims and their hidden victimisation at the hands of men was brought into sharp focus; women were introduced as offenders although their rates of offending remained much lower than those of men; and the maleness of offending was raised as a problem for the first time, fostering critical enquiry into the nature of masculinity and its links to offending (Cain 1990). As we have seen earlier, however, feminists had to struggle to change the perspectives of many male criminologists, both mainstream and critical in their outlook, who remained stubbornly blind to issues of gender in their work (Carrington 2002). Cain (1990) proposed that a wholesale transgression of criminology's boundaries was needed before the discipline could become sensitive to gender and that the entire criminological project should be deconstructed and reconstructed using the insights of women who could, after all, reveal so much more about the impact of social control mechanisms and their gendered nature than men would ever understand from their own knowledge base alone.

Feminist criminologists continued to introduce new and exciting insights into the field of criminology even as their views continued to be marginalised and pigeonholed as 'women's issues' (Carrington 2002). In the 1980s major shifts took place in feminist theory which began to filter into criminology in the late 1980s and early 1990s (Daly and Maher 1998). This further cemented the importance of building theories which were based on the socio-cultural aspects of gender and its many manifestations rather than merely studying women as a separate biological sex category. The introduction of postmodern and poststructuralist analyses of women's lives meant that there was a growing attention to differential experiences within the category of 'woman', a problematisation of claims made as to the universality of feminist 'truths', a critique of first-world feminism as inattentive to issues of racialisation and colonialism, and an attention to the criminological and legal discourses which shape the experiences of women as they move through systems of criminal justice. Howe suggested that the work of the late Nicole Rafter was particularly important in moving feminist criminology into a fuller consideration of the ways in which gender was key to an understanding of the experiences of females who had broken the law (Howe 1994:140).

Researching into the area of women's imprisonment, Rafter called for a *gender-sensitive* reading of practices of imprisonment. Masculinist accounts of imprisonment, Rafter argued, had all but ignored the experiences of women and missed a consideration of the totalising effect of incarceration on the female prisoner's sense of self. They had missed too, she argued, the intersections of gender, race and class which shaped the diversity of the experiences of the incarcerated. Rafter revealed the impact of the layers of multiple frameworks and intersecting structures which served to discipline the bodies and minds of women who found themselves 'inside'. Rafter's work was largely historical in nature; however, she hoped that further empirical work conducted on the female experience of incarceration would help to generate a comprehensive theory of the punishment of women (Rafter 1980 in Howe 1994:138). Carlen (1983) did explore the more contemporary spaces of imprisonment using feminist theory and methodology to reveal the gendered experiences of women incarcerated in the late twentieth century. Carlen first chose a narrative approach to her research in which the stories told by 20 women in Cornton Vale Prison revealed much about the gendered nature of punishments meted out to female prisoners. Their experiences inside prison, she argued, were shaped by the shifting, incipient, yet pervasive social attitudes which first placed females in straitjackets and chains on the outside of the prison establishment and which contributed to their prospects of future incarceration. It was the stifling impact of these social conventions on life outside the prison gates which Carlen suggested was at the root of particularly punitive attitudes towards women in the courts and in the prisons.

Carlen's research revealed a number of aspects to the punishment of women which had previously lain unnoticed. She demonstrated that while much smaller numbers of females than males were incarcerated, nevertheless the courts can impose heavy penalties on female law-breakers, locking them up for minor, petty offences for which men would not have been placed in custody. In addition she found that a significantly greater proportion of women than men were imprisoned for not paying fines and that a higher proportion of women are remanded in custody awaiting trial for petty offences. Carlen reported the observations of one member of a House of Commons Expenditure Committee in the UK who reflected that remand appeared to have been used in a purely punitive way for women with no justification for its application and despite the low levels of 'risk' which women placed on remand generally presented to society (Carlen 1983:23). Her findings raised a number of important questions concerning the ways in which the criminal justice system operated where women were brought to be tried and judged. Furthermore her work raised key issues suggesting that incarcerating women for short periods of time could not be justified on the grounds of social defence, nor could it serve any rehabilitative purpose.[3] She revealed that women continued to be trapped in a more punitive and widely cast carceral net and held to different standards of behaviour than men even as the smaller numbers of women in custody had obscured this significant fact.

Pathways to crime: a gendered analysis of women's law-breaking

The 1970s had witnessed a significant focus on female law-breaking, much of which was initially empirical in its approach as the nature and extent of female law-breaking were subject to detailed scrutiny (Cernkovich and Giordano 1979). Two contrasting views emerged: one which held that women and girls were less likely to engage in law-breaking behaviour as a consequence of patterns of socialisation which moulded them into conformity and a consideration of others; and another which argued that these patterns had been disrupted by the growth of feminism and that this was reflected in increasing rates of female delinquency across the developed world (Adler 1975, Steffensmeier 1978). Each side of the debate was concerned with uncovering the similarities and differences between male and female deviance, whether there had been a real increase in the involvement of females in law-breaking acts and whether the nature of female law-breaking had changed in intensity and in its range – becoming more serious as a consequence. They were also concerned with whether an apparent increase in numbers of females brought before the courts was an artefact of changed reporting and recording procedures, or even a consequence of the growing interest in and concern about the behaviour of girls which had drawn attention to the existence of 'the female offender'. Both positions were largely based on empirical observations, on an analysis of available statistics pertaining to the numbers of offenders brought before the courts and on self-report studies largely conducted with juveniles and the emphasis was on counting the numbers involved and offering a largely descriptive account (Cernkovich and Giordano 1979).

From the 1990s, however, the poststructuralist feminist lens was directed at a different question and utilised a different set of methodologies. These feminist theorists were interested in exploring ways in which gender shaped women's patterns of law-breaking and the response of criminal justice institutions to those women and girls who came before the courts. Their studies revealed a particular and shared backstory to explain the law-breaking behaviour of women and girls which was gendered and qualitatively different to the aetiology of crime committed by males. For women and girls law-breaking was often linked to a lack of control and to vulnerability. More females than males in the criminal justice system, for example, present with problematic substance abuse and it is suggested that, certainly in many countries in the West, women may turn to drugs or use alcohol as a coping mechanism and as a form of self-medication where their lives are otherwise unbearable

(Inciardi et al. 1993 in Blanchette and Brown 2006:12). In addition women's law-breaking is rarely harmful to other individuals, it rarely involves physical violence and is less likely to be motivated by thrill-seeking, the search for status or aggression towards another person (Miller 1998). It has also been revealed that women often break the law for reasons related to a lack of any alternative legitimate means to provide food, clothing and other necessities for children and others for whom they care (Blanchette and Brown 2006:10–11, Carlen 1990). In addition the amounts stolen are often small, the law-breaking is frequent as their caring responsibilities continue and it is often committed alone. Furthermore their crimes are often hidden from others rather than shared and celebrated with friends (Campbell 2005). These are not crimes which are committed to impress; indeed, females often express great shame at their behaviour and remorse as a consequence of their actions (Steffensmeier and Allan 1996). In addition, females often report that they have committed a crime to 'please others', to show or win affection (Blanchette and Brown 2006:12) or out of love for another (Fleetwood 2014). Some studies have also suggested that females involved in serious law-breaking are likely to have been pressured into this by men although this has also been contested (Blanchette and Brown 2006).

In the early 1990s Kathy Daly (1992, 1994) revealed her 'pathways to crime' analysis which set out to explain the ways in which gender defines and proscribes the behaviour of women and girls prior to their involvement in law-breaking. Daly's research was developed as a criticism of mainstream criminology which continued to assert that male and female law-breaking could be understood using the same existing theoretical tools but she also challenged the radical feminist perspectives which maintained that female offenders should be considered first as victims of male violence and control. Daly sought the 'middle-ground' (Wattanaporn and Holtfreter 2014:192), arguing for a more complex and nuanced understanding of the manifest patterns of female offending. Daly's pathways analysis revealed that women's pathways to crime, the frequency and nature of their offending and their patterns of desistance from crime all differ from men's equivalents (Bloom, Owen and Covington 2003, 2004). Despite her rejection of a crude characterisation of the female offender as a product of her previous victimisation, Daly argued nevertheless that there were gendered contexts to female law-breaking and that prior victimisation could be a relevant risk factor. Daly named four specific categories of law-breaking in which prior victimisation was relevant and these she named the street woman, the battered woman, the harmed and harming woman and the drug-connected woman. For all these categories Daly found there to be a history of gender-based factors where physical and sexual abuse and/or coercive control at the hands of men had featured heavily in the lives of these female law-breakers. Only the fifth category, the economically motivated woman offender, did she consider as free of such gendered pressures.

Trauma, victimisation and law-breaking

Daly's work has been much utilised within criminology and many have added further empirical and theoretical insights to her work (Wattanaporn and Holtfreter 2014). These writers (often female) highlight the correlation between abusive experiences and subsequent law-breaking and violent behaviour (Belknap 2001). While male offenders may also have experienced abuse in their past, these writers argue the data consistently demonstrates that more females than males have experienced abuse prior to their detainment and that this abuse has been more serious. In addition, the abuse which females have suffered is of a different order in that it is linked to the general oppression of women which is inescapable and any abuse is consequently more deeply and permanently damaging (Cauffman 2008). This abuse can take many forms and can be physical, sexual and psychological in character, leaving its victims severely traumatised and in need of therapeutic support (Chesney-Lind 1987, Heimer and De Coster 1999). This trauma can affect the ability of women to function successfully in many aspects of their lives. In the most serious manifestations of trauma-induced behaviours, research has revealed that women who kill do so for different reasons than men and that this is often linked to their own prior experiences of victimisation. When women kill within an intimate relationship, for example, it is very often after they have experienced years of abuse from their partners which is often endured silently and without their seeking help from support services (Belknap 2001). While much of the research that has been conducted on the impact of the violent victimisation of women and girls has been conducted in the West there is a growing recognition that this is a global problem, with some studies revealing that one in four girls aged between 15 and 19 years of age have suffered physical abuse and that one in ten girls worldwide have been subjected to serious sexual violence, much of which will have been persistent, although the majority will never have reported it (Chesney-Lind 2015:73).

The damaging effect of social controls on women and girls

The social controls which all females, and especially girls, are subject to can also leave them more vulnerable to abuse. Research has continued to reveal that controlling behaviour can be normalised within familial relationships, leading to the normalisation and acceptance of coercive abuse which is endured as simply 'the way things are' (Dougherty 1998). As a consequence women may live for years within controlling, violent or abusive relationships without speaking out or indeed recognising their situation as damaging to their self-esteem or physical and mental health. There is evidence to suggest that girls may be particularly damaged by a chaotic and disruptive family life, especially where the relationship between parents and child is emotionally poor (Chesney-Lind 1987). Research has similarly revealed that females who have come to the attention of the criminal justice system are more likely than males to exhibit poor mental health. This lack of psychological resiliency can also be linked to the forms of control to which girls are subjected and which keep them isolated within the home. Males are encouraged to find their meaning and place outside of the home, engaged in the public sphere, whereas females are still expected to find their role and fulfilment within the private and domestic sphere of family and intimate relationships. Girls and women will consequently face more of a struggle in difficult and dysfunctional families. Where domestic situations are lacking in love, care and empathy, this may be more deeply felt by females and therefore it has been argued that girls are more likely to be affected by intergenerational transmission of emotional and behavioural problems (Heimer and De Coster 1999).

Inserting the concept of gender-specific treatment into the justice system

Researching women's pathways into crime has revealed the interconnections between the gendered risk factors which contribute to much law-breaking by women. Poor family relationships, childhood victimisation, running away from home, prostitution and drug use have been found to be inextricably linked to women's law-breaking behaviour (Blanchette and Brown 2006:12). Women's pathways to crime mainly include a history of abuse, substance misuse, economic marginality and poor family dynamics (Belknap and Holsinger 2006, Daly, 1992, 1994, Steffensmeier and Allan 1996, Wattanaporn and Holtfreter 2014). As a consequence of these findings it has been suggested that their pathways out of law-breaking too may be similarly gendered. They have also raised questions as to whether women should be subjected to the same types of punishment as men, or whether gender-specific models which take account of women's specific vulnerabilities and their gendered pathways to crime should be envisioned and put into effect.

The 'pathways to crime' framework has proved particularly salient to the development of models of 'treatment' for girls and women who have broken the law which are sensitive to gender and which map out different models of working with females sentenced by the courts. The research has contributed to a perspective which is typified by the words of Katherine Van Wormer in her statement that:

> The reason that a gendered approach is crucial to the treatment of females within the criminal justice system is because girls are different from boys – physiologically, psychologically, and socially, and in more or less the same way, women are different from men.
>
> (Van Wormer 2010:2)

The theoretical insights of the pathways to crime model have been utilised in very practical ways to develop a number of alternative models of working with females who have been charged and convicted of committing criminal offences. The development of treatment and punishment programmes for women has become increasingly important as more women are caught by the criminal justice net and directed into 'facilities and interventions already designed with males in mind' (Van Wormer 2010:15). The proponents of gender-specific services have argued that women and girls have 'special needs' and that available services need to be tailored with those needs in mind.

Theorising punishment for women: a 'women-wise penology'

While empirical research was continuing to uncover the realities of women's experiences of the formal criminal justice system and was highlighting significant areas of concern, feminist academics were at the same time trying to understand the nature of punishment and to understand whether penal regimes should be adapted to incorporate women's experiences or replaced altogether. Attempts to understand and reconceptualise punishment from a feminist perspective were not attempted until the late 1980s at the time that Carlen (1989) wrote a short, but much-cited piece which called for a *women-wise penology*, one that could redress the discrimination faced by women within penal practices which had been shaped by patriarchal attitudes and the use of essentialised gender stereotypes. Carlen suggested that a fundamental principle driving this reimagining of penal policies and practice should be that women with experience of the criminal justice system should be allowed a voice in the design and running of the penal institutions in which they were placed. Carlen further suggested that, unlike previous regimens of punishment, a women-wise penology should be careful that alternatives do not increase women's oppression *as women*. In addition she was clear that the new penology should recognise men's role in the oppression of women and ensure that the punishment of men should not reinforce their oppressive attitudes and behaviour towards women. In this sense then the call was for a reimagining of punishment which would take into consideration not only sex differences but more so the extant gendered relations of power and control which are produced and reproduced in society and regimens of punishment and treatment of 'deviant' women.

Carlen's call for a 'women-wise' penology incorporated the idea, developed in the second wave of feminist activism and theory, that 'women's knowledge', the separate and distinct 'women's ways of knowing', should also be employed in the search for a solution. Carlen's approach was mirrored by Howe in her 1994 publication *Punish and Critique: Towards a Feminist Analysis of Penality*. Carlen and Howe, echoing earlier work by Carol Smart, called for the development of a distinctive feminist jurisprudence which would address 'fundamental issues like legal logic, legal values, justice, neutrality, and objectivity' (Smart 1984:66). These advocates of a feminist jurisprudence were inspired by 'the promise of a fully integrated theoretical framework and political practice which will be transformative' (Smart 1984:66). They rejected approaches which would involve merely tinkering with a system which ultimately, they believed, could not deliver anti-oppressive practice for women. Instead the feminist jurisprudence would offer 'a general theory of law which has practical applications' (Smart 1984:66). It was important for these theorists therefore that practice followed the theory and that a feminist theory of law had to be developed before effective practice could be imagined and instated into policy and procedure.

Carlen (2002) was clear that ample evidence existed to demonstrate that justice systems were, and are still, heavily gendered so that women are punished differently to men, women and girls are often placed into custody unnecessarily and the expansion of female imprisonment should be closely interrogated and probably could not be justified. The origin of this difference in treatment, however, was fiercely debated by feminist lawyers and criminologists. For liberal feminists inequalities in the legal system were a function of male dominance over the discipline and could be addressed through recognising the law's inattention to women's needs and the enactment of legislation which could make access to the law a more equal process. From the outset the proponents of liberal feminism sought to change existing laws to make them more female-friendly and to enact new ones which could protect women and legislate around their particular needs. Others, such as the radical feminist MacKinnon (1983), Olsen (1995) and Smart (1986), however, were profoundly sceptical of this approach which they considered could only produce marginal benefits for women.

Formal equality paradigm: treating women the same as men

The most basic right which feminists have had to fight for is the right of women to be considered as equal social actors to men. Within the existing legal framework it has been considered imperative that women be considered as full 'persons' in law, as capable and rational beings who are deemed fit to bear responsibility, and not be classed alongside children, animals and inanimate objects which are considered unfit to bear personal responsibility for their actions (Naffine 2011). As we have seen previously, however, for many centuries females were treated as less than fully human and rendered subject to the will of males, without the means to challenge their treatment or to choose a different path. When the legal status of females is not considered equal to that of males then the chances of women and girls obtaining equality and justice are severely limited. Many jurisdictions still maintain, for example, that the testimony of females cannot be held equivalent to that of males or uphold discriminatory laws governing the family which give power over women to the male and presumed head of the household. These are systems where patriarchal systems are still deeply enshrined within social and legal frameworks. Feminist activists across the globe have argued that it is imperative to challenge these ideas in order to begin to ensure female equality and attain any kind of justice for women. The fight for equal status and parity of treatment for women has been a significant call amongst feminist activists worldwide.

The equality paradigm therefore starts with the need to treat women on the same terms as men. It requires a *formal equality* within the law with men and women subject to the same laws, equally applied regardless of sex. It is a liberal concept which demands consistency of application of the law so that 'like must be treated as like' (Barnard and Hepple 2000). However, there are a number of limitations to this formal equality paradigm. Three key elements to this paradigm raise fundamental issues which question its appropriateness to the position of gender-sensitive perspectives:

- It is a procedural principle so the law is interpreted to the letter without concern for the consequences for those to whom the law is applied.
- It is a relative principle which requires that there are at least two groups, one of which must be compared to the other in order to test whether equality has been delivered. It therefore perpetuates a distinction, in this respect between the categories of male and female, which is considered of fundamental importance.
- It is a symmetrical principle so it does not guarantee a favourable outcome for either group as both may be treated equally badly. Likewise, it may result in the worsening of a particular group's condition as the group treated comparatively better than another may have this preferential treatment challenged and they may lose their privileges.

Treating men and women with formal equality therefore does not guarantee a favourable outcome. It represents a position based on the understanding that all those brought before the courts should be judged as equivalents and does not take into account the differential circumstances and gendered constraints which shape individual behaviours. Neither does it recognise that the same treatment might lead to very different outcomes depending on the individual circumstances of the person to whom judgement is applied. The principle is gender-blind, arguing that the law should be applied to all regardless of their sex and related personal circumstances. Neither does this approach address the masculinist nature of law and punishment which assumes the presence of a male body, forcing women into regimes which were developed to constrain the male subject. White gives the example of women being issued with men's uniforms in prison – the treatment was the same but disadvantaged women considerably, as they were forced to wear clothing which was ill-fitting, uncomfortable and stripped them of any connection to their female embodiment and so robbed them of their essential humanity and sense of self-worth (White 2012).

The need for a comparator is also a source of concern. Consider the condition of pregnancy and maternity where there is no comparison in the male condition. Men, as current science allows, simply cannot become pregnant, carry a child to term or give birth and suckle. While paternity is a key moment in many men's lives it simply is not the same as the birth mother's journey over the months of pregnancy, the act of birthing a child and then the intimate and deeply physical relationship which the mother and child will share for many months afterwards. As a consequence there is no possibility of ensuring equity to the expectant or actual mother as the formal equality paradigm cannot rule on equal treatment under these circumstances (Ferdinand and McDermott 2002). The formal equality approach has also been used to argue *against* any treatment which is specific to women's condition, and by which men could not equally benefit, declaring such specialised treatment as an injustice to men (Ritter 2003:8).

Despite these problems the principle that females should enjoy legal rights to the same standard as males has been recognised as an important step on the road to achieving equality. As Hudson (2003:35) argued, 'Criminal law has been very slow and very resistant to allowing in the feminine imaginary' and for centuries proved an inadequate tool for recognising and then addressing the victimisation of women at the hands of their 'protectors'. Certainly overturning centuries of jurisprudence which denied women their legal rights is an essential turning point in the history of any system of law. However, it has been argued that a 'strategy based solely on the acquisition of legal rights using "male" rights as a standard may provide benefits for women that are more symbolic than actual' (Saksana 2007:484) and this recognition shaped an alternative imagining of what equality is and how it could be attained.

Substantive equity: equal but different

The critics of the formal equality approach looked for a more transformational model by which women might win equal justice. They argued that in the construction of the law as it was formulated under patriarchy, the concept of the 'legal person' set up a standard which all those looking to achieve such status have to emulate without consideration of the significance of difference and diversity (Naffine 2011). These writers considered that legal systems which had been made by men and for men were therefore inherently flawed and could not be reformed in a piecemeal fashion to incorporate the needs of women. Instead justice had to be reconceptualised along feminist lines and the 'man-made' law needed to undergo a wholesale revision of legal systems before it could deal with the complex issues related to the structural violence and oppression which were the undoing of the female sex (Naffine 1990). The very principles on which law was founded, in its adversarial nature, its emphasis on free-will and the rational man of enlightenment thought, as well as in its understanding of the distinction between public and private, they argued, all mitigated against the incorporation of the female experience which was more complex and variable and which was tainted by structural inequalities which contributed to both institutionalised and personalised discrimination against the female sex (Easteal 2001). While equal rights campaigners were eventually successful in extending legal personhood to women, forcing courts to treat women as independent decision-makers in the same way as men were treated, on its own this move could not ensure that the law became gender-neutral and equally of use to males and females. As Ritter (2003) reveals, legal frameworks still use men's 'condition' as the norm and the standard by which women are measured.

Instead they argue for an approach of *substantive equality* wherein difference is recognised, fully considered and accounted for and which recognises that women have different and specific experiences which need to be taken into consideration in order that they are not disadvantaged by a legal system which has been developed with the male condition as its normative framework and to which women are compared and often found lacking. This position takes equality of outcome and parity in treatment as the goals to be pursued, firmly rejecting the idea that sameness somehow delivers equality. Revisiting Ferdinand and McDermott's example from earlier, this position would accept pregnancy as a woman-specific condition which requires a woman-specific response and consequently the extension of employment insurance to pregnant women. Evidence is emerging that *gender-specific* treatments can be particularly effective for female offenders, especially when this takes account of and targets the multiple aspects of the lives of women and girls who break the law. Such treatment, it is argued, is sensitive to the diversity within women's experiences, is clear that female offenders are not a homogeneous group and argues that treatment ultimately should be tailored to suit individual needs defined more specifically than by gender alone (Cauffman 2008:119).

Reformist or *radical* change?

The debate between formal and substantive equality feminists has been cast as between a liberal, reformist tradition which argues that the modern legal systems offer a progressive opportunity which should be adapted to include women's specific needs and priorities, and a more radical standpoint within feminism which suggests that the corruption of the legal system by patriarchy is so deeply embedded that the system as a whole must be entirely transformed. The formal equality theorists, however, have responded by questioning the wisdom of perpetuating the view that there are fundamental differences between men and women. Theorists such as MacKinnon (1983) have argued that this reinforces a set of essentialised stereotypes on which patriarchy thrives. The position of difference, they argue, perpetuates the idea that women are vulnerable creatures in need of state and familial protection, different from men and therefore requiring a different set of standards, rights and protections which cannot be shared equally between the sexes. Difference should be de-emphasised and similarities re-emphasised and the principles of sameness embedded into the treatment of women inside and outside the criminal justice system. To suggest that women have unique vulnerabilities, they argue, casts women in a poorer light, robs them of their moral agency and suggests that they are incapable of independent thought and action.

The two positions outlined here remain hotly contested within feminist debates. The position of *gender-sensitive* treatment is much more closely allied with the perspective of substantive equality which has underpinned many of the models of gender-sensitive treatment programmes and models of custodial practice. It is to the development of these principles which we turn in the following chapter.

Notes

1 In the UK the police were put under pressure in the early 2000s when it came to light that a number of historical and current cases of organised sexual abuse of minors (mainly girls) had been allowed to continue despite the girls' reporting of their attackers. The testimonies of the young girls involved had simply been dismissed or they were held responsible for the abuse due to their 'promiscuity'. In 2002 the Metropolitan Police suggested that all such allegations should henceforth be believed and in 2005 a report by Her Majesty's Inspector of Constabulary affirmed that this position should be taken and that at the initial reporting a belief in the victim should be institutionalised and an investigation immediately follow. Only 11 years later the Metropolitan Police commissioner, Bernard Hogan-Howe, suggested that this had been a mistaken policy which had not protected the falsely accused. The initial policy was instigated to protect the innocent, vulnerable yet unbelieved (mainly females). It appears that by 2016 the balance of power was swinging back in favour of the accused (mainly men) (Hogan-Howe 2016).

2 Chesney-Lind and Okamoto (2001:2–3) pointed to a 50.3 per cent increase in the numbers of girls arrested in the US between 1989 and 1993 which compared to a 16.5 per cent increase in the number of boys arrested. Arrests of girls for serious violence increased by 64.3 per cent and for 'other assaults' by 125.4 per cent.

3 Carlen (1989) reports that in 1980 over 60 per cent of adult women sentenced to prison in England and Wales received sentences of six months or less, with the average custodial sentence in Scotland in 1978 being 74 days for women over the age of 21.

References

Adler, F. (1975) *Sisters in Crime: The Rise of the New Female Criminal*. New York: McGraw Hill.

Barnard, C. and Hepple, B. (2000) 'Substantive equality', *The Cambridge Law Journal*, 59(3): 562–585.

Becker, H. (1967) 'Whose side are we on?', *Social Problems*, 14(3): 234–247.

Belknap, J. (2001) *The Invisible Woman: Gender, Crime, and Justice*. London: Wadsworth.

Belknap, J. and Holsinger, K. (2006) 'The gendered nature of risk factors for delinquency', *Feminist Criminology*, 1(1): 48–71.

Blanchette, K. and Brown, S.L. (2006) *The Assessment and Treatment of Women Offenders: An Integrative Perspective*. Chichester: John Wiley.

Bloom, B., Owen, B. and Covington, S. (2003) *Gender-Responsive Strategies: Research Practice and Guiding Principles for Women Offenders.* Washington, DC: USDOJ, National Institute of Corrections.

Bloom, B., Owen, B. and Covington, S. (2004) 'Women offenders and the gendered effects of public policy', *Review of Policy Research*, 21(1): 31–48.

Cain, M. (1990) 'Towards transgression: new directions in feminist criminology', *International Journal of the Sociology of Law*, 18(1): 1–18.

Campbell, A. (2005) 'Keeping the "lady" safe: the regulation of femininity through crime prevention literature', *Critical Criminology*, 13(2): 119–140.

Carlen, P. (1983) *Women's Imprisonment: A Study in Social Control.* London: Routledge and Kegan Paul.

Carlen, P. (1989) 'Crime, inequality and sentencing', in Carlen, P. and Cook, D. (eds), *Paying for Crime.* Milton Keynes: Open University Press, pp. 8–28.

Carlen, P. (1990) *Alternatives to Women's Imprisonment.* Milton Keynes: Open University Press.

Carlen, P. (2002) *Women and Punishment: The Struggle for Justice.* Cullompton, UK: Willan.

Carrington, K. (2002) 'Feminism and critical criminology: confronting genealogies', in Carrington, K. and Hogg, R. (eds), *Critical Criminology: Issues, Debates, Challenges.* Cullompton: Willan, pp. 114–142.

Cauffman, E. (2008) 'Understanding the female offender', *The Future of Children*, 18(2): 119–142.

Cernkovich, S.A. and Giordano, P.C. (1979) 'Delinquency, opportunity, and gender', *Journal of Criminal Law and Criminology*, 70(2): 145–151.

Chesney-Lind, M. (1982), 'Guilty by reason of sex: young women and the juvenile justice system', in Price, B.R. and Sokoloff, N.J. (eds), *The Criminal Justice System and Women.* New York: Clark Boardman, pp. 303–322.

Chesney-Lind, M. (1987) 'Girls and violence: an exploration of the gender gap in serious delinquent behavior', in Crowell, D., Evans, I. and O'Donnell, C. (eds), *Childhood Aggression and Violence: Sources of Influence, Prevention, and Control. Applied Clinical Psychology.* New York: Plenum Press, pp. 207–229.

Chesney-Lind, M. (1995) 'Girls, delinquency and juvenile justice: toward a feminist theory of young women's crime', in Raffel Price, B. and Sokoloff, N. (eds), *Women, Crime, and Criminal Justice.* New York: McGraw Hill, pp. 71–88.

Chesney-Lind, M. (2015) 'Gendered pathways into delinquency', in Cullen, F., Wilcox, P., Lux, J. and Johnson, C.L. (eds), *Sisters in Crime Revisited: Bringing Gender into Criminology.* Oxford: Oxford University Press, pp. 83–102.

Chesney-Lind, M. and Okamoto, S. (2001) 'Gender matters: patterns in girls' delinquency and gender responsive programming', *Journal of Forensic Psychology Practice*, 1(3): 1–28.

Cohen, A. (2016) *Imbeciles: The Supreme Court, American Eugenics, and the Sterilization of Carrie Buck.* London: Penguin Press.

Daly, K. (1992) 'Women's pathways to felony court: feminist theories of lawbreaking and problems of representation', *Southern California Review of Law and Women's Studies*, 2: 11–52.

Daly, K. (1994) *Gender, Crime, and Punishment.* New Haven, CT: Yale University Press.

Daly, K. and Maher, L. (1998) 'Crossroads and intersections: building from feminist critique', in Daly, K. and Maher, L. (eds), *Criminology at the Crossroads: Feminist Readings in Crime and Justice.* New York: Oxford University Press, pp. 1–20.

Dougherty, J. (1998) 'Power-belief theory: female criminality and the dynamics of oppression', in Zaplin, R. (ed), *Female Offenders: Critical Perspectives and Effective Interventions.* Gaithersburg, MD: Aspen Publishers, pp. 165–196.

Easteal, P. (2001) *Less than Equal: Women and the Australian Legal System.* Chatswood, NSW: Butterworths.

Ekholst, C. (2014) *A Punishment for Each Criminal: Gender and Crime in Swedish Medieval Law.* Leiden: Brill.

Farrington, D. and Morris, A. (1983) 'Sex, sentencing and reconviction', *British Journal of Criminology*, 23(3): 229–248.

Ferdinand, T.N. and McDermott, M.J. (2002) 'Joining punishment and treatment in substantive equality', *Criminal Justice Policy Review*, 13(2): 87–116.

Fleetwood, J. (2014) *Drug Mules: Women in the International Cocaine Trade.* Basingstoke: Palgrave Macmillan.

Freedman, E.B. (1981) *Their Sisters' Keepers: Women's Prison Reform in America, 1830–1930.* Ann Arbor: The University of Michigan Press.

Garland, D. (1990) *Punishment and Modern Society: A Study in Social Theory.* Chicago, IL: University of Chicago Press.

Heimer, K. and De Coster, S. (1999) 'The gendering of violent delinquency', *Criminology*, 37(2): 277–318.

Hogan-Howe, B. (2016) 'Suspected sex offenders have rights the police must respect', *The Guardian*, 10 February, www.theguardian.com/commentisfree/2016/feb/10/accused-sex-crimes-anonymous-until-charged-reputations-police-complaint [Accessed 11 March 2016].

Holdsworth, E. and Hucklesby, A. (2014) 'Designed for men, but also worn by women', *Criminal Justice Matters*, 95(1): 14–15.

Howe, A. (1994) *Punish and Critique: Towards a Feminist Analysis of Penality.* London: Routledge.

Hudson, B. (1997) 'Punishment or redress: current themes in European abolitionist criminology', in MacLean, B.D. and Milanovic, D. (eds), *Thinking Critically about Crime.* Vancouver, BC: Collective Press, pp. 131–138.

Hudson, B. (2003) *Understanding Justice: An Introduction to Ideas, Perspectives and Controversies in Modern Penal Theory.* Buckingham: Open University Press.

MacKinnon, C. (1983) 'Feminism, Marxism, method and the state: towards a feminist jurisprudence', *Signs*, 8(4): 635–658.

Miller, J. (1998) 'Gender and victimisation: risk among women in gangs', *Journal of Research on Crime and Delinquency*, 35(4): 429–453.

Naffine, N. (1990) *Law and the Sexes: Explorations in Feminist Jurisprudence.* London: Allen and Unwin.

Naffine, N. (2011) 'Liberating the legal person', *Canadian Journal of Law and Society*, 26(1): 193–203.

Newman, G.R. (1978) *The Punishment Response.* Piscataway, NJ: Transaction.

Olsen, F. (ed) (1995) *Feminist Legal Theory.* Aldershot: Dartmouth.

Peters, R. (2005) *Crime and Punishment in Islamic Law: Theory and Practice from the Sixteenth to the Twenty-first Century.* Cambridge: Cambridge University Press.

Pollak, O. (1950) *The Criminality of Women.* Philadelphia: University of Pennsylvania Press.

Pollock-Byrne, J. (1990) *Women, Prison and Crime.* Pacific Grove, CA: Brooks/Cole.

Rafter, N.H. (1985) *Partial Justice: Women in State Prisons, 1800–1935*. Boston, MA: Northeastern University Press.

Ritter, G. (2003) 'Women's citizenship and the problem of legal personhood in the United States in the 1960s and 1970s', *Texas Journal of Women and the Law*, 13(1): 1–40.

Romero, R. (2014) 'Beginning to give voice to a great silence', *Magdalene Laundries Testimony*, http://magdalenelaundrytestimony.org/ [Accessed 21 March 2016].

Ruggles, S. (1983) 'Fallen women: the inmates of the Magdalen Society asylum of Philadelphia, 1836–1908', *Journal of Social History*, 16(4): 59–82.

Saksana, A. (2007) 'CEDAW: mandate for substantive equality', *Indian Journal of Gender Studies*, 14(3): 481–498.

Smart, C. (1984) *The Ties That Bind: Law, Marriage, and the Reproduction of Patriarchal Relations*. London: Routledge and Kegan Paul.

Smart, C. (1986) 'Feminism and law: some problems of analysis and strategy', *International Journal of the Sociology of Law*, 14(2): 109–123.

Smart, C. (1989) *Feminism and the Power of Law*. London: Routledge.

Steffensmeier, D. (1978) 'Crime and the contemporary woman: an analysis of changing levels of female property crime, 1960–1975', *Social Forces*, 57(2): 566–584.

Steffensmeier, D. (1980) 'Assessing the impact of the women's movement on sex-based differences in the handling of adult criminal defendants', *Crime and Delinquency*, 26(3): 344–357.

Steffensmeier, D. and Allan, E. (1996) 'Gender and crime: toward a gendered theory of female offending', *Annual Review of Sociology*, 22: 459–487.

Van Wormer, K. (2010) *Working with Female Offenders: A Gender-Sensitive Approach*. Hoboken, NJ: John Wiley and Sons.

Walter, I. (1999) *Transgressing Gender? A Study of Girls in Gangs*. PhD Thesis, London South Bank University.

Wattanaporn, K. and Holtfreter, K. (2014) 'The impact of feminist pathways research on gender-responsive policy and practice', *Feminist Criminology*, 9(3): 191–207.

White, G.D. (2012) 'Gender-responsive programs in U.S. prisons: implications for change', *Social Work in Public Health*, 27(3): 283–300.

Williford, M. (1975) 'Bentham on the rights of women', *Journal of the History of Ideas*, 36(1): 167–176.

Chapter 3

Gender-responsive justice in action

The rise of gender-specific justice

The concept of 'gender-specific' justice has scored some remarkable successes in gaining attention outside of academia, and it has been widely endorsed and adopted in many different ways and in the practice of a number of organisations and criminal justice systems. In many ways the move to adopt gender-specific justice practices has from the start been practitioner-led rather than theory-based and flowed from the concerns of criminal justice professionals working with women who experienced a lack of fit between existing provision for females and the women and girls who were referred to them. The beginnings of gender-specific justice can be traced to a series of practitioner-led meetings which took place in the US in the 1980s under the rubric of the Adult and Juvenile Female Offenders Conference. These meetings have been described as:

> A grassroots movement [which] began to provide a forum for corrections professionals to come together every other year and share information and concerns regarding the needs, services and treatment of women and girls involved in the justice system.
>
> (Association for Justice-Involved Females and Organizations 2016)

The first such conference took place in 1985 in Minnesota and they have continued as biennial conferences ever since. The first meeting was given the title 'The Risk of Innovation: Moving the Establishment', the second in North Carolina 'Fitting the Pieces Together; Female Offender Dilemma' and by the fifth year and third conference, which was hosted in Pittsburgh, Pennsylvania in 1989 and titled 'Changing Needs of the Female Offender: A Challenge for the Future', the organisers and participants were calling for 'a fundamental restructuring of corrections for women' (Correctional Service of Canada 1990).

Canada was the first country to adopt national policy which reflected the concerns of the 1989 Pittsburgh conference. In 1990 the Correctional Service of Canada (CSC) published a report *Creating Choices: The Report of the*

Task Force on Federally Sentenced Women which 'proposed the development of a culturally appropriate, woman-centred model of corrections' (Hannah-Moffat 2002:199). The report was the culmination of a year-long *Task Force on Federally Sentenced Women* which was set up to look at the management of 'federally sentenced women' from the moment of sentence to the point at which the woman was discharged from the service's care.[1] The task force was co-chaired by the Canadian Association of Elizabeth Fry Societies and the CSC. It was charged with working in partnership with other organisations to develop a future guide to the national correctional process which, it was emphasised, '*is responsive to the unique and special needs of this group*' (Correctional Service of Canada 1990 [italics in the original]). From the outset, then, the Canadian government promoted a women-centred perspective which took the view that women as a group faced problems and experiences which were not shared by the male population. The members of the task force listened directly to the testimonies of incarcerated women, and maintained that 'It was federally sentenced women themselves who gave us the energy and determination to create a new vision; a vision based on choices' (Correctional Service of Canada 1990). The willingness of the authors of the report to listen to, and to act upon, women's accounts of pain and suffering which they endured in the supposed 'care' of the state is a notable feature in many a policy report which has recommended that significant changes are required in the ways that females are managed within the processes of criminal justice. The narratives of women have acted as powerful drivers of change in the move to re-perceive women who break the law as something more than merely 'offenders' and to reimagine the ways in which society should respond to this particular group.

In the US the idea of providing gender-specific services within criminal justice was raised in 1992 by the chair of a hearing for the US House of Representatives charged with reauthorising the Juvenile Justice and Delinquency Prevention Act. According to Chesney-Lind and Okamoto this was to become a landmark hearing in the US and was the first time that the provision of services to girls was raised as an issue of concern. The hearing was concerned with the high numbers of girls who were arrested for welfare or 'status', rather than criminal, offences and the high numbers who violated court orders and the question was put as to why there were no alternatives other than youth jail available for girls (Chesney-Lind and Okamoto 2001:14). As a direct consequence of these hearings the reauthorised act specifically required that each state undertake an analysis of gender-specific services noting the availability of such services but further requiring that each state look into the need for such services and to plan to provide them in the future. Additional money was made available for the development of gender-specific services and 23 states took up the challenge – with what Chesney-Lind and Okamoto describe as 'ominous' results for girls; however, the call for gender-specific programmes was now on the table in the US as well.

Only two years later, in December 2000, the idea of gender-specific services went global with a commitment 'to develop action-oriented policy recommendations based on the special needs of women as prisoners and offenders' enshrined in a United Nations (UN) resolution which was later strengthened by draft rules, formulated in Bangkok in 2009, calling for the provision of gender-specific health-care, mental health and rehabilitation programmes within custodial and community settings. Since the start of the twenty-first century the literature on gender-specific justice and its practice has exploded with hundreds of articles published in academic journals and policy reports advocating the turn to gender-specific approaches. It would appear therefore that the 'gender-specific turn' was finally complete. It is important, however, to look more closely at the detail of the programmes provided under this rubric and to scrutinise what exactly has been achieved under the label of gender-specific justice.

The global reach of gender-specific justice

The late twentieth century was a remarkable period for the growth of knowledge and interest in the lives of girls and women. In the development of women as a legitimate area of study we see the initial phase of thinking which was to lead to the call for a sensitivity to gender in policy and practice. The serious exploration of women's lives brought to global attention the multi-faceted oppression which women face as women and which is specific to the workings of gendered social relations. Demands were made that this gender-specific oppression should be recognised and challenged everywhere. For too long, it was argued, society had been gender-blind, unaware and uncaring of the impact of oppression on women's lives. A growing body of evidence produced by activists and academics alike had demonstrated that what had been considered as gender-neutral practices were in actuality blind to the needs of women and girls and demonstrated the predominance of an androcentric perspective which at best pushed women's experiences into the margins and at their worst often harmed women and girls in the process. The call for the development of gender-specific justice practices was taken up with some enthusiasm by the UN during this period and the UN has done much to disseminate the ideas and practice of gender-specific programming across the global stage. This championing of a gender-specific perspective began in their recognition that women were denied the full range of their human rights' entitlement and in the concern that this should be addressed as a global priority.

CEDAW, the UN and a global focus on women and gender

In 1979 the UN General Assembly adopted the Convention on the Elimination of all Forms of Discrimination Against Women (CEDAW) which it describes on its website as 'an international bill of rights for women' and which set out to define and to eliminate all forms of discrimination against women (UN 2009a). Any member state which ratified the principles of CEDAW was thereafter legally committed to abolish discriminatory laws, adopt laws which prohibited discrimination by individuals, private or public bodies and to ensure that public institutions protected women against discrimination. The UN considered it necessary to set up CEDAW as they argued that 'the fact of women's humanity [had] proved insufficient to guarantee them the enjoyment of their internationally agreed rights' (UN 2009b). It was therefore agreed that the setting up of a separate convention and ongoing support for the Commission on the Status of Women were necessary in order to continue UN work on achieving the full range of human rights for all women. Although CEDAW was adopted in a shorter period than any other human rights legislation put forward by the UN, suggesting it had widespread support, it is also one of the most heavily reserved treaties in the UN human rights system with many countries applying for reservations on traditional, religious and/or cultural grounds, thereby 'spread[ing] the view that ratifying CEDAW is less binding than other human rights treaties' (Saksana 2007:484).

Despite its shortcomings the UN focus on gender during the latter part of the twentieth century, and indeed since, has played a significant role in advancing the arguments of advocates for women's rights across the globe. CEDAW has been heralded as recognising the importance of promoting a model of *substantive equality* (see Chapter 2) and as such has been useful in applying pressure on governments and legislative bodies to make substantial changes to positively benefit women and girls (Salime 2011). CEDAW has also helped to highlight gender-based violence and to aid in the recognition of what have become known as 'gender crimes'; those crimes which are perpetrated against women because they are women such as sexual slavery or mass rape in times of war or those crimes which are perpetrated disproportionately against women such as domestic violence and sexual assaults (MacKinnon 2011:17). CEDAW has also been seen by many feminists as a useful tool for activists to employ to allow them to continue to expose discrimination and to ensure that a dialogue concerning the need for gender justice is sustained (Saksana 2007). However, the Convention has also faced criticism from many quarters. While laying out the principles underlying the need for legal equality for women, feminists have argued that it has not been able to change the structures of oppression which daily discriminate against women and girls and which remove fundamental rights and opportunities from their grasp. CEDAW has also been critiqued as furthering 'ethnocentric, philosophical beliefs' which are incompatible with legal and cultural norms in many countries around the globe. In addition it has been argued that CEDAW perpetuates the ghettoisation of women's issues, suggesting that women's concerns are somehow separate from universally held declarations of human rights (Saksana 2007: 484–495).

Gender mainstreaming

In the late 1980s the term 'gender mainstreaming' entered the global policy vocabulary to refer to a strategy through which it was suggested that gender equality could be better achieved in practice if it was required consideration in the development of all policies. The idea of mainstreaming gender acknowledged the criticism that women's issues were being ghettoised and furthermore that considering women's rights separately to the general human rights frameworks which were being developed would sideline key gender-related issues and would ultimately prove to be to the detriment of females. In 1975 the UN sponsored the World Conference of International Women's Year which took place in Mexico and which kick-started the UN Decade for Women. This 1975 conference has been heralded as a significant 'catalyst for attention to women's issues … around the world' (Alston 2006:125). The UN focus at that time was mainly in ensuring that women were fully included in development projects which would ensure their economic independence individually and the sustainability of their communities more generally. However, towards the end of the Decade for Women an evaluation of UN development projects concluded that projects which specifically targeted women were less successful than those which were considered as mainstream but that included an element which demanded a sensitivity to gender. The evaluations concluded that 'attention to the differences between the roles, responsibilities, and opportunities of women and men increases the probability that projects will involve and benefit women' (Carloni 1987:xiii). By 1995 gender mainstreaming was established as a transnational and global issue when it was fully endorsed at the UN's Fourth World Conference on Women in Beijing (Alston 2006). The Platform for Action which was produced from that meeting stipulated that:

> In addressing the inequality between men and women in the sharing of power and decision-making at all levels, Governments and other actors should promote an active and visible policy of mainstreaming a gender perspective in all policies and programmes so that before decisions are taken, an analysis is made of the effects on women and men, respectively.
> (UN 2001a:1)

Henceforth the UN stipulated that service-providers should reflect on the extent to which their work was blind to issues of gender and the resultant impact on women. It was made incumbent on service-providers not only to redesign services and systems to remove their harmful effects for the female sex, but to ensure that new projects recognised women's particular needs and values as of equal significance to those of men. Gender-mainstreaming was not about developing separate women's projects or women-specific elements to existing services but instead required that the consideration of gender and its impacts be made central to all activities, not just in the delivery of services but also in their implementation, in their monitoring, in research, design and development (UN 2001b). This shift in thinking did not entail the abandonment of programmes and resources targeted specifically to women, indeed these were considered as an essential additional and complementary strategy which would be necessary until gender equality was achieved, but it has been seen as a 'radical alteration of the processes and structures which reproduce women's subordinate position' in many key institutions (Bhatta 2001:28 cited in Alston 2006:129).

The Bangkok Rules

The ideas of gender-sensitivity and gender-specific needs which gained currency during this period emerged initially in the health and development sectors but were later adopted across a wider area of concerns and more specifically in the ways in which women were treated within their respective criminal justice systems. As early as 1980 the *Sixth United Nations Congress on the Prevention of Crime and the Treatment of Offenders* had adopted a resolution which called on countries to recognise the specific problems which women face in prison and had called for the development of non-custodial alternatives for women and girls. This call was reiterated in the seventh, eighth and ninth congresses and the tenth further asked member-states to explore and address any disparities in the impact of crime prevention programmes on women and men. In 2010 the UN finally approved *The Bangkok Rules* which laid out specific standards 'for the treatment of women prisoners and non-custodial measures for women offenders' (UN 2010). Again the UN had become mindful of the fact that their Standard Minimum Rules for the Treatment of Prisoners, adopted in 1955, 'did not draw sufficient attention to women's particular needs' (Harm Reduction International 2016). The Bangkok Rules stressed the need to apply gender-specific measures to women and encouraged all member-states to prioritise non-custodial sanctions for women and girls wherever possible. They were concerned with the vulnerability of women to institutional practices which might result in further harm to women and also with the impact of incarceration on dependent children who were not responsible for the decisions of their parents but who would be emotionally and psychologically scarred by their incarceration. The Bangkok Rules openly acknowledged that many prison facilities had been designed for male prisoners and that they were not suitable for the particular needs of the female inmate. By this point the UN's commitment to considering the special needs of women in systems of criminal justice was firmly established. The Bangkok Rules called for the basic principle that women prisoners had 'distinctive needs' and that providing for these was not discriminatory. The 70 rules stipulated the following areas where women should be considered differently to men.

On admittance to prison – Particular care should be taken at the time of a woman's admittance to prison, paying regard to their particular vulnerability at that moment. It was suggested that women were less familiar with the processes of imprisonment and of in-prison regulations. It was also suggested that women should be allowed time to make arrangements for the care of their children before being detained even if this meant suspending detention for a period of time. Women should be able to express a preference as to which prison they would be admitted to and this should take into consideration any request to be close to their home, dependants and community of release.

Caring for their dependent children – The details of all dependent children and their care arrangements should be kept by the prison facility into which the woman was admitted. In addition any children accompanying their mothers to prison should also have access to health specialists, appropriate services and access to their mothers for as much time as possible. Removal of children should only be allowed if it is considered to be in the best interests of the child. Women with children, or who are pregnant or breastfeeding, should have their specific nutritional needs catered for.

Physical and mental health – Facilities should take into consideration women's specific hygiene needs, with free access to sanitary products and a regular supply of water to ensure their personal care needs are satisfied. There should be comprehensive health-screening of all women in prison especially regarding their mental health-care needs, reproductive health, drug-dependency and histories of sexual abuse or violent victimisation and they should have their medical records kept strictly confidential. Women should have access to gender-specific health-care and preventative health-care services and be treated by a female medical specialist wherever possible. Male prison staff should only be in attendance when this cannot be avoided. Mental-health services should also be sensitive to gender and trauma-informed. Prison staff should be cognisant at all times of women's stress and deal with this sensitively and strategies should be developed to avoid suicide and self-harm.

Recognition of past traumas – Women who have suffered abuse and violence should be informed of their rights to take legal action against the perpetrator, be given assistance to take this forward and be offered specialised counselling and support services. In addition measures should be taken to ensure that the woman is kept safe from any subsequent retaliation. Women's dignity and respect should be ensured at all times with personal searches only conducted by appropriately trained female staff and alternatives such as body scanning should be available. Segregation should not be applied to women with children or to pregnant women. Women who report abuse should be provided with immediate protection, support and counselling and their claims investigated promptly and taken seriously.

Family contact – Care should be taken to ensure that women have regular contact with their families and that where children visit this should take place in an appropriate environment. Women should also be consulted as to whom they would bar from visiting. Discipline should never involve the withdrawal of contact with family and women should never be restrained during labour or immediately after giving birth.

In-prison regimes – Staff working with women prisoners should be fully trained in caring for and working towards the rehabilitation of the women under their care. Classification of women prisoners should also be gender-specific, taking into consideration the lower risk which women prisoners pose to others and the women's prior victimisation and rehabilitative needs. Women in prison should have access to a full range of activities which are appropriate to their gender and their particular individual needs. Foreign nationals, minority and indigenous women should have their distinctive cultural needs met.

On release – Prison authorities should work with community services and organisations to develop and implement effective reintegration programmes which should begin before release and continue afterwards.

Alternatives to custody – Women should not be placed in custody inappropriately with particular attention paid to policies which place women on remand and the use of referrals to protective custody outside the prisons should also be scrutinised to ensure that women are not being dealt with more punitively at this stage. Courts should be careful when sentencing women, and parole boards when considering release, to ensure that they take into consideration mitigating factors such as the lack of a criminal history, the level of offending and caring responsibilities. Non-custodial alternatives should always be preferred for pregnant women, those with dependent children and female juveniles.

The Bangkok Rules were rights-based in their approach and covered the criminal justice process from courts to post-prison release. While general in their recommendations they persisted with the perspective of substantive equality: that women have special needs, that the context of their law-breaking should be considered at all times and that the social circumstances in which women and girls are placed have a bearing on the decisions which they make and the opportunities available to them. Despite the numbers of member-states signing up to these rules, however, the approach which they outline and the standards which they are set have been rarely attained, as we will see.

Gender-specific programming in criminal justice

While these important arguments were taking place on a transnational plane, the practice of gender-specific justice continued to be developed within organisations involved in criminal justice practice in different national contexts. Much early work on gender-specific criminal justice practices continued to be conducted within the North American context. In the US in particular the numbers of women coming into contact with the criminal justice system had noticeably increased, but more worryingly the ratio of females to males was beginning to alter, with numbers of women coming to the attention of the authorities increasing at a faster rate than the numbers of men (American Correctional Association 1993:v). By early 1992 the US-based *Federal Prisons Journal* had devoted an entire issue to the problems associated with housing females in institutions which had been predominantly designed and managed by men. In 1993, Gondles,[2] the Executive Director of the American Correctional Association (ACA),[3] while not using the term gender-specific, was able to state that:

> different programs for different needs are necessary, and administrators at all levels are beginning to share and discover the best ways to handle female inmates and their particular concerns.
>
> (American Correctional Association 1993:v)

Many of the articles published within this special edition were written by practitioners working within the US 'corrections' industry as prison wardens, administrators, researchers and prison chaplains, and grappling with the 'problem' of working with sentenced and incarcerated women on a daily basis. They reflect a real concern with the welfare of the women under their care and a situated knowledge of their needs which had been based on a close and sustained relationship with incarcerated women. As a consequence they reflected a willingness to develop a constructive and women-informed approach to their work and to pass this knowledge on to others so that meaningful reforms could be made to settings which had hitherto been particularly damaging to women. These practitioners were adding to the knowledge-base and were infused with an optimistic viewpoint which held that reshaped and reformed interventions could really make a difference to the lives of incarcerated women inside the carceral institutions into which they had been placed and subsequently in their 'rehabilitation' into society.

In Canada the pressure for change was even more palpable and appeared to be felt and heeded at the highest levels (Hannah-Moffat 1991). Despite decades in which the Federal Prison for Women had attracted a significant amount of attention and criticism for maltreating its inmates, the reception of the report *Creating Choices* in 1990 appeared to herald a real change. Much of the evidence collected in the report was qualitative in nature and drawn from the narratives of the women incarcerated. A particular strength was the report's attention to the needs of Aboriginal women inmates, a group which was clearly over-represented inside the prison walls and which was subject to particular 'cultural ignorance and deprivations' (Hannah-Moffat 1991:194). The report was clear in its call for a complete overhaul of the 'corrections' system for women, which should be clearly led from the top and culminate in wholesale change, not 'the patchworking evident in so many correctional systems' (Correctional Service of Canada 1990:Chapter 3).

Despite its early promise, in the US progress towards gender-sensitive programmes has been rather more piecemeal. In 1993 Oregon became the first state to pass a bill which required state agencies working with juveniles to ensure that girls had equal access to appropriate services and facilities. Guidelines were drawn up which promoted an equity model in both the years 2000 and 2002 and which ensured that specific treatments were developed which were sensitive to the special needs of young females (Morgan and Patton 2002). In the decade that followed gender-specific programmes for women proliferated across the US; examples can be found within prisons (Calhoun et al. 2010) and post-release (Carlton and Segrave 2015), in substance abuse programmes for women (Messina et al. 2010, Prendergast et al. 2011), in probation (Gardner 2004) and almost every aspect of programmes for female law-breakers (Stalans 2009). Nevertheless, the US has not, as in Canada, implemented a nationwide strategy legislating for women's needs and subsequently a patchwork/piecemeal approach has been evident despite the fact that most evaluations of gender-specific programmes have been generally positive, acknowledging that women respond well to women-only and gender-specific environments.

In Australia and New Zealand there have been a number of gender-specific programmes implemented, again as a state-by-state initiative rather than driven from national policy requirements. Examples can be found from 2003 in New South Wales, then in South Australia (2004), Victoria (2006) and Western Australia (2006–2008). Tasmania, Australia's Northern Territory and various organisations in New Zealand have also acknowledged the need to develop diversionary programmes targeted at indigenous women. These programmes acknowledged that indigenous women were subject to higher rates of violence than other women, were over-represented as victims of crime more generally and that they experience discrimination on the basis of their ethnicity as well as their gender (Bartels 2010). These programmes, reflecting the direction of policy in Canada, have recognised the intersection of gender oppression and race discrimination in the lives of indigenous women and have argued that programmes need to be culturally relevant as well as sensitive to gender. They have included a significant input from grassroots organisations working for indigenous peoples such as 'Strong Sisters' based in Bunbury, Western Australia which have argued for protection of indigenous women from discriminatory policing practices which were based on an ignorance of the conditions under which many indigenous women live and which subjected them to negative stereotyping and over-policing as a consequence.

The programmes developed by Aboriginal women were therapeutic in their design. They acknowledged a history of the marginalisation, disrespect and denial of indigenous cultures and the invasion and continued occupation of their lands was recognised as a significant trauma to First Nations communities. The harms of colonisation were said to contribute to the over-representation of indigenous peoples in prison, added to the pains of imprisonment and affected the lived experience of indigenous peoples so severely outside of the prison walls that they were more likely to come into conflict with the law or to be targeted as a problem population by state authorities. The recommendations of the Canadian reports were therefore to close the existing prison for women, to construct smaller, regional facilities, to develop services and facilities which incorporated community expertise, using community volunteers where appropriate, and to get women out of prison as quickly as possible. Each facility would be well provided with a range of programmes which women could take up which would be based around their emotional, psychological, medical, educational and other needs, sensitive to their histories of abuse and able to teach a range of skills to help the women to survive their abuse and begin to thrive. An Aboriginal 'healing lodge' would also be built to allow Aboriginal women to serve their sentences in a space which would incorporate their own cultural norms and address their specific needs. Outside of these spaces of incarceration the Canadian government promised an expanded and strengthened network of community-based facilities built around similar gender-sensitive principles. Unfortunately the community-based organisations which were part of the development of culturally relevant programmes have faced significant funding cuts across both Australia and New Zealand over the last decade and the voices of the grassroots are increasingly being driven out of the conversation (Bartels 2010:10).

In the same year that Hannah-Moffat assessed the influence of gender-responsive criminal justice responses in Canada, across the Atlantic in Britain Beckett wrote that 'Gender is at the forefront of current government policy in the UK'. Her evidence was a series of new initiatives piloted in both Scotland and England which emphasised the importance of recognising the social circumstances that lead some women to break the law and the need to intervene early to ensure that women's needs can be met so that they would be less likely to resort to law-breaking. These initiatives were also designed to promote the use of community-based programmes and 'disposals', thereby shifting the penal culture away from punishment and towards rehabilitation and 'treatment' (Beckett in McIvor 2004:318).

In practice the UK government was somewhat slower in responding to calls for gender-specific and woman-centred justice than Beckett's quote suggests. Hedderman reports that, while promising a radical new approach to offenders in 1997, the then recently victorious Labour Government delayed any consideration of responding to female offenders until the establishment of the Women's Offending Reduction Programme (WORP) which was delayed until 2004 (Hedderman 2010). WORP was scheduled to run for an initial three-year period, tasked to develop a 'multi-agency strategic plan of action to deliver a distinct and joined-up response to the needs and characteristics of women offenders' in England and Wales (Home Office 2004:5). WORP's stated purpose was to reduce the extent of women's offending and to achieve equality of treatment and access to provision for women. Its aims were modest; indeed,

Hedderman argues, any radical impetus which might have initially lain behind the establishment of WORP had long been abandoned by the time it eventually started work (Hedderman 2010:489). While WORP set out to provide 'a better tailored and more appropriate response to the particular factors which have an impact on why women offend' (Home Office 2004:5), the programme was careful to make clear that it was 'about mainstreaming gender consideration rather than developing entirely separate systems and approaches for women offenders' and it was not, it clearly stated, about giving women offenders preferential treatment (Home Office 2004:14).

In Scotland, on the other hand, two reports *Women Offenders: A Safer Way* and *A Better Way: The Report of the Ministerial Group on Women's Offending* published in 1998 and 2002, respectively, paved the way for services tailored specifically to the needs of women offenders and resulted, amongst other outcomes, in the establishment of the 218 Centre in Glasgow which opened in 2003 a year before WORP came into being for England and Wales. In Scotland an emphasis was placed on alleviating the detrimental social circumstances that led some women to offend, on early intervention and on promoting punishment and treatment services which could be accessed within the community. The 218 Centre was established to provide residential and community-based resources to women assessed as particularly vulnerable to custody or reoffending and who might have a substance misuse problem, and was run by the voluntary sector organisation Turning Point, known for its expertise in working with people with drug and alcohol problems. The approach championed by the Scottish Executive was to support organisations which could provide specialist treatments which aimed to 'reduce stigma and isolation and increase confidence and self-esteem, improve social skills, alter criminal attitudes and behaviour and so engage with these women [who offend]' (Scottish Executive 2002; see also Scottish Executive 1998).

The Home Office for England and Wales delayed until 2006 before it moved further in the agenda set out by WORP. At this point it engaged Baroness Jean Corston to 'conduct an independent review of "vulnerable" women offenders and other vulnerable women who come into contact with the police or courts, identifying gaps in provision for their needs within the criminal justice system and related health services' (Corston 2007:90). As a result of her review Corston recommended a radical, new woman-centred approach to working with criminal justice-involved women which would treat women both holistically and individually. She also recommended a fundamental rethinking of the way services for women are provided in the community. Furthermore, Corston suggested moving planning and delivery of services for women who offend or are at risk of offending away from the Home Office (by then renamed the Ministry of Justice) and into the Department of Communities and Local Government, suggesting that the government's focus should be 'more closely aligned to the community agenda' and should be delivered from outside of what she regarded to be a highly gendered criminal justice system

(Corston 2007:7). The government formally accepted much of what Corston recommended and in 2008 a National Service Framework for working with women offenders was drawn up, a guide to working with women offenders was published and in addition the Criminal Justice Women's Unit was set up to manage and coordinate the response to Corston. In addition further funding was found in 2009 to extend the model of women's centres which Corston had recommended as an exemplar of practice and which followed the model of Scotland's 218 Centre (Hedderman, Palmer and Hollin 2008). Unfortunately 2010 saw a change in government in the UK. Thirteen years of an administration led by the Labour Party ended in May that year when Britain's first coalition government in decades came into being – a partnership between the Conservative and Liberal Democratic parties. This government immediately announced a period of austerity in which government funds were severely limited and embarked on a strategy of the privatisation of criminal justice and prison services. With funds to the women's centres lost and a fragmentation of criminal justice provision, the vision of WORP was soon lost and with it the commitment to continue to support a policy direction which was gender-sensitive in its perspective.

Despite the slow pace of reform and its piecemeal nature in many administrations, in 2008, nearly 20 years after *Creating Choices* was published, Hannah-Moffat could argue that after 30 years of research, policy development and programmes designed to reflect the female experience, the models of gender-responsive correctional, rehabilitative and treatment services were 'rising to the ascendancy' and taking their rightful place alongside more traditional, masculinist and risk-based discourses (Hannah-Moffat 2008:194).

Gender-specific programming in practice

In 1998 two US-based academics Barbara Bloom and Stephanie Covington presented a paper to the American Society of Criminology entitled *Gender-Specific Programming for Female Offenders: What is it and Why is it Important?* This paper, which has been much cited, set out the principles of the approach as they saw it developing in practice, as did a subsequent edited volume *Gendered Justice: Women in the Criminal Justice System* (Covington and Bloom 2003). These publications brought the practice of gender-specific justice into academic consideration whilst the principles which they outlined as guiding gender-sensitive practice have also acted somewhat as a blueprint for further practice in the area. Indeed in their 1998 paper Bloom and Covington set out their concern to take the conversation on gender-specific services away from the more theoretical and abstract and towards its applications in practice in order to ensure 'that promising program models can be presented to criminal justice practitioners and policy makers' (Bloom and Covington 1998:1). Their work therefore set out to inform both theory and practice.

Reflecting a growing academic interest in the subject and in the practical application of gender-sensitive work, Bloom and Covington raised a concern that there was no 'clear definition and statement of guiding principles and criteria' for what they termed 'gender-specific services' (Bloom and Covington 1998:7). This reflected the practitioner-led design and delivery of gender-specific services for women and girls. In the absence of any such statement they suggested the following principles should be adopted:

- equality does not mean sameness; in other words, equality of service delivery is not simply about allowing women access to services traditionally reserved for men – equality must be defined in terms of providing opportunities which are relevant to each gender. Thus, treatment services may appear very different depending on to whom the service is being delivered;
- gender-specific programs are not simply 'female-only' programs that were designed for males;
- females' sense of self is manifested, and develops differently, in female specific groups as opposed to co-ed groups;
- the unique needs and issues (e.g. physical/sexual/emotional victimization, trauma, physical and mental health, pregnancy and parenting) of women and girls should be addressed in a safe, trusting and supportive women-focused environment;
- whenever possible, women should be treated in the least restrictive programming environment available. The level of security should depend on both treatment needs and concern for public safety;
- treatment and services should build on women's strengths/competencies and promote independence and self-reliance; and
- cultural awareness and sensitivity should be promoted and the cultural resources and strengths in various communities should be utilized.

(Bloom and Covington 1998:9–10)

This 'holistic' approach has subsequently become a mainstay of gender-specific models of work with women. It fits with the feminist values of woman-centred practice and the approach of substantive equality. Developing a holistic perspective was clearly linked to the perceived need to understand and address a historical legacy of discrimination and oppression of the female sex which had left women and girls with low levels of self-esteem and a lack of confidence in their abilities, which had tied them into highly dependent relations on men and stripped away their means for self-sufficiency. They suggest treatment options which are non-hierarchical, which are therapeutic in their design and which see women in their entirety rather than merely as subjects of penal policy. They are trauma-informed, recognising women's prior experiences of harm and discrimination and they are also relational in that they see the female as closely connected to wider social networks which impact on their lives in significant ways and which can be used to help the individual heal. The principles of gender-sensitive justice were developed to distance gender-sensitive provision from the paternalistic treatment of women which existed up until the 1970s, in which female offenders in the system were infantilised in institutions and denied equality in employment, and which built on a double standard in sentencing practices which culminated in closer control of girls. However, while women-centred they are not overtly feminist and allow for the development of legislation, policy and service provision which are gender-based but not driven by a feminist philosophy (Van Wormer 2010:18).

Barriers to the implementation of gender-specific services

Even when the general principles have been accepted there remain many barriers to the implementation of approaches which are sensitive to women's needs in the criminal justice system. The gender-sensitive approach was developed during a period when recorded crime rates in many countries reached a high point, crime became highly politicised as an issue especially during electoral periods and in reaction the numbers of juveniles, women and men incarcerated across the globe increased substantially. The 'penal populism' which resulted (Hughes 2007) has meant that while funds have been found for policing and prison-building the support for rehabilitation and reintegration has been less than forthcoming (Gideon 2011). The economic and social context in which the criminal justice system is expected to function has also undergone significant changes. The data consistently shows that the majority of people who come into contact with the criminal justice system remain some of the most marginal in society – poorly educated, poorly housed, struggling with their mental health, unable to find decent employment and trapped in poverty (Gideon 2011). Unemployment in many countries has remained stubbornly high as short economic booms have been followed by longer slumps in economic activity and while global productivity may have increased, the share of the world's wealth which is distributed to the poorest in society has not kept pace. Neoliberal economics and politics have ensured that many countries which are struggling to develop their national economic base have been held back by debt, unable to translate their increasing prosperity into much-needed educational, employment and housing infrastructures which would help lift their populations out of poverty and a precarious existence. So while efforts have been made to absorb the principles outlined by the proponents of therapeutic, holistic interventions for those at risk of coming into contact with the criminal justice system, the wider context has not been conducive to such a move.

As we have seen in Chapter 1, criminal justice and penal institutions across the globe have been guided by a very different set of principles which are in reality fundamentally incompatible with those which have been associated with gender-specific justice. The requirement to punish has continued to dominate the field, and from the 1980s there has been an added impetus to justify massive state expenditures on criminal justice and to demonstrate the effectiveness of that expenditure using actuarial techniques and the assessment of 'risk' – an agenda which has been named the *What Works?* approach. In addition a push towards deterrence and incapacitation has meant that the goal of rehabilitation has been pushed much further down the line. This has been all too apparent within the US criminal justice system but is not limited to that particular national jurisdiction. While the states of Northern Europe in particular have resisted these pressures to varying extents, the rhetoric of toughness can be heard across most regions of the globe even as different states and localised authorities introduce and experiment with a different set of approaches. The following sections look at the impact of the *What Works?* agenda which predominated after the 1970s and which required that all expenditure on criminal justice interventions be closely monitored and evaluated, and look at the application of risk-based assessments to the 'correction' of individual law-breakers which emerged in the 1990s.

Does *What Works?* work for women?

In 1999 Bloom and Covington presented a further paper to a largely academic audience at the American Society of Criminology annual meeting which they titled *Gender-Responsive Programming and Evaluation for Females in the Criminal Justice System: A Shift from What Works? to What is the Work?* In the 12 months between their papers a shift in emphasis becomes obvious. The 1999 paper moved away from a simple outline of the principles of gender-specific justice to suggest a paradigmatic shift in criminological thinking was necessary in order for gender-specific, now named 'gender-responsive', justice to be realised in practice. This shift, they argued, should follow a shift which had taken place in the natural sciences from seventeenth-century Newtonian to twentieth-century quantum physics (from a system of logical empiricism to one of socio-rationalism). In criminology this meant abandoning the search for a 'cause and effect' model which could account for law-breaking and its replacement with a 'whole-system' approach which recognised the effects of systemic and structural violence on the lives of those brought before the systems of criminal justice. Bloom and Covington argued for a replacement of the *What Works?* evaluator frameworks which had dominated criminology since the mid-1970s and a move to a different kind of assessment of criminal justice interventions which was informed by 'a science based on holism, scientific thinking, and interconnection' (Bloom and Covington 1999:6). The mechanistic and reductionist *What Works?* model, they concluded, could never measure the effectiveness of interventions designed specifically for working with women and addressing their multiple needs. The only positive effect which was deemed worthy of measurement for *What Works?* was the rate of recidivism and a related drop in crime-rates. They argued that for women, however, an absence of the continuation of law-breaking behaviour might be the least effective measure which could be chosen to gauge an improvement to their life chances and subsequent opportunities to break free from harmful and self-destructive behaviours.

What Works?, it has been argued, is based on a masculinist view of where risk is centred (Hannah-Moffat 2002). The law-breaking of males, it is argued, is likely to involve harm to others and therefore it might make sense for male law-breakers to be considered as a significant risk to the community and for the extent of that risk to be measured by diagnostic and other tools. According to this logic the 'risky individual' must then be appropriately managed and controlled in order that the risk to others can be minimised and society in general be protected. The law-breaking of women, however, as we have seen in Chapter 2, is more likely to result in harm done to the woman herself, rather than to any other individual. In these circumstances, where women are the subject of any intervention, the notion of 'risk' should involve a very different focus which should not be based solely on reducing the individual law-breaker's capacity to harm others, but also on reducing their capacity to further harm themselves. In addition the background of women who break the law is so often one of historical and ongoing trauma and victimisation that the clearest way to prevent further victimisation is to attend to the woman's needs, to work with her, to lift her out of the circumstances which contributed to her law-breaking, to strengthen her confidence and resilience so that she can better counter the attacks upon herself and to remove the triggers which expose her to situations of vulnerability. It is important also to consider how the masculinist mentality of 'corrections' and imprisonment reproduces women's trauma and victimisation so that there is no respite from it while in state custody for the female who is re-traumatised and re-victimised by the very systems which are put in place to 'correct' and 'manage' her behaviour, so daily reproducing the conditions which contributed to her law-breaking in the first place (Belknap 2001).

Bloom and Covington understood the importance of the systemic and structural factors which contributed to women's law-breaking; their paper was critical of individualised assessment instruments which place the responsibility for law-breaking on personal characteristics alone, and they were scathing in their critique of narrowly framed evaluations of criminal justice practice. Bloom and Covington also argued for a shift in approach from the perspective of cognitive psychology which focuses on the individual and the expert's assessment of their capabilities, to relational psychology which understands that the person can only be understood by reference to the networks which sustain (and can harm) them. They considered relational psychology as more appropriate for understanding women's position in societies which attribute individualistic rationalism to the male yet emotionality, sentiment and interpersonal connection to the female. Putting new science, socio-rationalism and relational psychology at the centre of the criminal justice system, would, Bloom and Covington opined:

> shift the discussion … to looking holistically and systemically at women in the context of their life history, as well as acknowledging the connection between social policy and criminality. (Bloom and Covington 1999:10)

In many ways their paper could be read not only as an attempt to develop a different methodology for working with women which places them in the totality of their life experiences, but also – in their call for a paradigmatic shift in approach – as their attempt to find a different language through which to express the female experience. As we will see in Chapter 5 this novel perspective which they were beginning to formulate at the time, however, has been subsequently absorbed into the very language and practice of the masculinist risk-based approach which they had set out to critique and contest. At this point, however, Bloom and Covington added to their 1998 paper a further set of guiding principles for what they were now referring to as 'gender-responsive' work. The 'work' they said was to include the following principles:

- Prevention – to put facilities in place in the community which would lower the risk of women becoming criminal-justice involved. This would include economic support, responding to violence against women and the provision of facilities to support women who were abusing drugs and alcohol.
- Do no harm – all procedures should be scrutinised and where they are perceived to be perpetuating harmful practices they should be removed or significantly modified. Alternatives to custody should be created, staff should be trained to treat women with respect and held to account if they are abusive.
- Gender-responsive services should be created – which take account of the systemic inequalities faced by women, not just the individualised factors which might contribute to a woman's law-breaking. Her poverty, race and culture should also be considered as significant issues.
- Community support should be built – resettlement services should help women to obtain housing, employment, childcare, transport and so forth so that women can settle more easily back into their community.

A different set of evaluative principles

Bloom and Covington's recommendation of a paradigmatic shift also encompassed a turn away from narrow conceptions of *What Works?* in terms of recidivism to argue that evaluative processes should involve *Appreciative Enquiry* (Dosher and Terry 1993 in Bloom and Covington 1999:13), developing a collaborative and participatory evaluation framework which involves all programme participants working towards an appreciation of the strengths and resources encompassed within a service and which harnesses the knowledge gained to action improvements to the future delivery of the programme. The importance then is not to measure outputs and certainly not to measure 'success' on the basis of individual outcomes but to enable staff and others to reflect on their service and envision ways in which it could be bettered. Bloom and Covington argued that evaluation should not be used merely to improve a particular programme but for the assessment to encompass the context in which the programme operates and to attempt to change that context in order to allow a particular intervention to be effective. They recognised a need for transformational leaders who can offer 'a possibility of hope and transformation that extends beyond the women themselves to the criminal justice system and society at-large' (Bloom and Covington 1999:15).

What Works? evaluations are clearly distinguishable from and incompatible with those *Appreciative Enquiry* methodologies preferred by Bloom and Covington in 1999, for:

> The former insists that we cannot begin to address the needs of girls in the juvenile justice system until we understand the sociological and systemic forces that carry them to its doorstep. The latter emphasizes the individual differences that influence girls' responses to these sociological forces and determines whether they will choose an antisocial or pro-social pathway.
>
> (Hubbard and Matthews 2008:229)

Furthermore, *What Works?* evaluations take a gender-neutral stance, considering criminogenic factors to be shared by male and female alike, whereas Bloom and Covington's methods are informed by a feminist praxis, the view that women's experiences demand a different ontological and epistemological approach, that the complexities of gendered oppression cannot be understood and accounted for by a masculinist and ultimately oppressive framing of effect, efficiency and measurable outcomes. It is concerning then that it is difficult, however, to detect the principles of *Appreciative Enquiry* in many subsequent evaluations of programmes aimed at addressing women's needs. The indicators of success most often used are still those which are informed by the *What Works?* paradigm, that is, that there is a search for evidence of a reduction in recidivism and other narrowly defined outcome-based measures. While the gender-responsive components of interventions are acknowledged they are generally not considered as measurable in these terms so are not included as evidential findings – and this despite the fact that there is 'no shortage of assessments to use as a guide for measuring fidelity to gender-responsive principles' (Salisbury, Van Voorhis and Spiropoulos 2009:7). There has also been a push to find a way to reconcile the two very different approaches (Hubbard and Matthews 2008) but in practice *What Works?* principles are much more in evidence in evaluations.

There are, nevertheless, numerous accounts of the benefits of therapeutic programmes which consider the circumstances which most convicted law-breakers endure (Gideon 2011:6–10). These acknowledge the difficulties encountered within communities where work is scarce, where finance is hard to come by, where many are denied access to even the most paltry of benefits and in which those exiting from criminal justice systems are labelled as 'offenders' and face particular difficulties in gaining respect and inclusion. These accounts recognise the importance of educational and vocational training, ongoing treatment for addiction and interventions which are based around recognition of the strengths and abilities of those convicted. However, more punitive approaches and narrow measures based on numbers of crimes committed or re-entry numbers to prison are still considered more effective. These hard quantitative evaluative measures are favoured above the qualitative and richer accounts of the experiences of 'softer', more therapeutic approaches and in the final analysis:

> funding is spent on hiring more prison staff, constructing new prisons, and meeting the rising costs of health care, leaving very little funding for treatment and work programs. As a result, not enough money is left to fund these supportive programs. Despite the knowledge that these programs can be effective, legislators continue to withdraw funding for re-entry initiatives, leaving prisoners to be released into a situation that is many times worse than what they experienced before they entered prison.
> (Gideon 2011:14)

Gender-responsive programming: the incorporation of gender into the mainstream?

As indicated already, Bloom and Covington shifted their vocabulary from one of *gender-specific* to that of *gender-responsive* programming in 1999. The terms gender-sensitive, gender-specific and gender-responsive have often been used interchangeably in the ensuing years to describe a range of policies and interventions that encompass a 'woman-centred approach' and which begin from the premise that the special needs of girls and women are real in their effects and need to be taken into account (Van Wormer 2010:15). However, it is worth reflecting further on the emergence and salience of the term 'gender-responsive' and to reflect on the effect which the emergence and general use of that term may have subsequently had on a wider comprehension as to what the approach actually entails in practice.

In the 1980s a number of criminal justice researchers based in the US and engaged in the problem of *What Works?* began to work on developing a theory as to why 'some offenders benefit more from certain types of treatment provided by certain types of therapists' (Bonta 1995:1). According to their frame of reference, whatever worked for one 'offender' should work for all; after all, they were interested in discovering the universal principles on which all 'correctional' institutions could rely. Their conclusion was that not all offenders are the same and that 'individual offenders can be identified by their intelligence, communication style and emotionality' which subsequently have an influence on how they 'respond' to the treatment offered and to 'efforts to change their behaviour, thoughts and attitudes' (Bonta 1995:1). These researchers developed the notion of a 'responsivity principle' which would require 'correctional' staff to deal with offenders, not as a homogeneous group, but as individuals who would react to any intervention in ways which were specific to their character. They also argued that the character and attitudes displayed by particular members of staff were key to a successful intervention, concluding that empathetic, 'warm, interpersonally skilled therapists' were most likely to be effective (Bonta 1995:2).

It is hard to take issue with the idea that the relationship between staff and service-user is an important factor in any intervention. As we have seen, the proponents of what were now termed as gender-responsive interventions considered an environment of empathy, respect and understanding as key to the healing process. However, Bonta's understanding of the relationship differs markedly from that which was envisioned within gender-responsive principles. Bonta's model is not strengths-based but an individual deficit model. He argues that 'offenders' differ from 'the general population' in that they have poorer social and verbal skills, inadequate problem-solving capacities, that they are more 'concrete-oriented' in their thought processing and 'have little internal motivation to change' (Bonta 1995:2). He concludes that the best approach to working with offenders is that of 'structured cognitive behavioural treatment' which must set clear behavioural goals, providing opportunities for success but presumably also marking as a failure those who do not achieve the targets set. Individual 'traits' such as anxiety and low self-esteem, poor mental health and gender, race and age, he considers as shared with the general population and requiring to be taken into consideration as 'needs'. However, Bonta employs clear categorisations which separate 'criminogenic' from 'non-criminogenic' needs. Criminogenic needs, such as substance abuse, increase the 'likelihood of criminal conduct' whereas non-criminogenic needs – and he specifically points out low self-esteem as within this category – do not. Where needs are not linked to law-breaking then they 'are simply individual attributes that affect the achievement of treatment goals' but should not be considered as risk factors or as treatment goals (Bonta 1995:2–3). So it was not the goal of these programmes to address any of the non-criminogenic factors – gender included. As Bonta argued in this framework, 'there is no convincing evidence that addressing these [non-criminogenic] factors … will lower recidivism' (Bonta 1995:3). This can be seen as an example of the classic, masculinist logic and empiricist thinking which Bloom and Covington rejected. In the intervening years, however, the use of the preferred term of *gender-responsivity* has suggested that there is a connection between these two ways of thinking which is simply not present. Bonta does make concessions to feminist, indigenous and cultural theories in affirming that:

> Another important set of responsivity factors may be gender, race and ethnicity. Programming sensitive to gender and cultural issues may, therefore, enhance treatment effectiveness. For example, feminist-oriented groups for female offenders and healing circles for aboriginal offenders provide a context for increasing motivation and targeting criminogenic needs.
>
> (Bonta 1995:4)

However, Bonta has already made clear that these are secondary factors whose inclusion is aimed at making the individual more receptive to the main goal of addressing their own deficits in order that they can more easily reintegrate into the general population. There is no fit here with the principles which Bloom and Covington outline, nor any shift away from the old masculinist paradigms which have driven thinking heretofore. The concessions to feminist and cultural considerations are devoid of a real understanding of the significant issues which had been raised over the preceding two decades. Indeed Bonta specifically rejects non-behavioural relationship-oriented approaches as contributing far less to reducing levels of recidivism although it is these which underpin Bloom and Covington's gender-responsive alternate.

The Risk-Needs-Reponsivity model which was finessed by Bonta and his associates from the early 1990s has taken a prominent position in 'corrections' programmes across the US. This model enjoys a continued prominence, prioritised above programmes which cannot demonstrate an impact on reducing recidivism (Salisbury, Van Voorhis and Spiropoulos 2009:553–554). It claims to be gender-neutral (Holfreter and Cupp 2007), yet the model has been heavily critiqued as developed for men using men's experiences as the yardstick, as being inappropriate for women and as over-assessing the risk which women and girls who break the law pose to the population as a whole (Bloom, Owen and Covington 2003, Chesney-Lind 1997, Van Voorhis and Presser 2001); nevertheless, it continues to be applied to women in all kinds of 'correctional' settings. It uses both the language and tools of actuarial risk assessment to classify and 'correct' women and men who have been convicted of law-breaking (Salisbury, Van Voorhis and Spiropoulos 2009). It is employed in many community-based programmes and has been assessed as contributing to effective programmes to reduce offending. Its approach fits well within a political environment in which years of 'war on crime' rhetoric have culminated in a characterisation of the 'offender' both as outside of the norm and as a danger that must be closely controlled and scrutinised. This perspective has been felt particularly keenly by women and girls who have subsequently been arrested, convicted and imprisoned in much greater numbers as a consequence of their being equally assessed as a danger and risk to others (Belknap 2001, Steffensmeier et al. 2005).

Despite the incompatibility between Risks-Needs-Responsivity (RNR) models and those which Bloom and Covington outline as gender-responsive, there has been, as we have seen with the *What Works?* approaches, a general move to adapt the former in order that they might incorporate a meaningful element of response to gender. It has been suggested that women should be added into the assessment instruments used through the inclusion of risk-related research on women and demonstrating that issues such as trauma, low self-esteem, dysfunctional relationships, parenting responsibilities and so on affect women disproportionately and in different ways to men, and to reclassify these as criminogenic factors for girls and women (Salisbury, Van Voorhis and Spiropoulos 2009). It has been argued that 'had we started with women, the current generation of risk or needs assessments might look quite different from the status quo' (Salisbury, Van Voorhis and Spiropoulos 2009:557) and this is undoubtedly true if we look at the approach which Covington and Bloom outlined. However, as the future direction of gender-responsive programming reveals, the design of treatment programmes for women has become closer to RNR models while RNR models have not moved to incorporate gender-sensitive logics and approaches. In the final analysis RNR and gender-sensitive programmes remain incompatible, built as they are on different sets of principles and perspectives. Masculinist logics have resurfaced as dominant and tainted the delivery of programmes to women and girls.

The National Institute of Corrections in the US has worked with a number of different organisations and individuals who are concerned with getting things right for girls and women and they have developed a number of tools such as the *Women's Risk and Need Assessments*, the *Women's Case Management Model* and the *Gender-Responsive Policy and Practice Assessment*, all of which claim to be gender-informed policies, practices, assessment and training programmes designed to guide agencies in examining how each agency delivers services to women and to help them identify where improvements should be made (Buell 2015:16, Covington and Bloom 2006). They have borrowed from the literature on gender-responsive approaches to require assessment of the environment, staffing, management and classification of women, to scrutinise the services and programmes offered and to evaluate in such a way as to ensure that they meet the needs of gender-responsive programming. These can look to the outside observer as though they are meeting the goals of gender-responsive treatments but this strategy of adding women into the mix ignores the call for a paradigmatic shift in our thinking which would steer us away from the existing mentality of 'corrections' and towards a very different understanding and assessment of women's needs.

A lost age of innocence?

Worral and Gelsthorpe (2009) have argued that the ten years before the 1989 Philadelphia conference represented a point of almost 'lost innocence' during which criminal justice professionals and academics appeared united in a critique of the ways in which social and criminal justice policy discriminated against women and when national discourses on women offenders appeared to reflect the concern to make women visible and to listen to ways in which services could be improved for this group. Since then, they argue, the 'risk' agenda has grown to dominate discussions concerning work with offenders and as a result, while isolated projects were still conscious of gender in their practices and aimed to develop progressive tools to work with women, the domination of managerialism and the *What Works?* agenda has distorted the delivery of the majority of services to those labelled as offenders.

The vocabulary of criminal justice programmes for women has changed since the turn of the century to incorporate the agenda of risk and responsiveness to risk. The language of 'women-centredness' or sensitivity to gender has been pushed aside and the more abstract model of 'gender-responsivity' has taken centre-stage. Any examination of gender-responsive programmes in action reveals the difficulties in sustaining alternative and feminist approaches to working with women and girls in the context of the masculinist and 'risk-crazed' discourses which currently dominate critical justice policy-making (Carlen 2008) in many regions of the globe. These difficulties will be returned to and re-examined in the following chapters.

Notes

1 At the time there were only around 260 women incarcerated by the federal system in Canada which represented around 2 per cent of the total federally sentenced prison population. Around half of the women had been placed in the only federal prison for women in Canada, a maximum-security facility. The rest were placed in provincial prisons. Many were therefore placed far from their homes and wrongly classified as high risk (Miller-Ashton 1993).

2 It should be noted that while James A. Gondles contributed to this call for women's needs to be taken into consideration, he came to the post of Executive Director for the ACA with a significant history of claims of sexual harassment of his staff against him (American Correctional Association 2016).

3 The ACA states on its website that it is 'a professional organization for all individuals and groups, both public and private that share a common goal of improving the justice system'. It currently has an international reach with members from Canada and Mexico (American Correctional Association 2016).

References

Alston, M. (2006) 'Gender mainstreaming in practice: a view from rural Australia', *National Women's Studies Association Journal*, 18(2): 123–147.

American Correctional Association (1993) *Female Offender: Meeting the Needs of a Neglected Population*. Baltimore, MD: United Book Press.

American Correctional Association (2016) 'Our mission', American Correctional Association, www.aca.org/ACA_Prod_IMIS/ACA_Member/About_Us/Our_Mission/ACA_Member/AboutUs/MissionStatement_home.aspx?hkey=7a39e689-8de2-47d4-a7d4-93cce9442142 [Accessed 1 April 2016].

Association for Justice-Involved Females and Organizations (2016) 'History of AJFO Conference', Association for Justice-Involved Females and Organizations, www.ajfo.org/about [Accessed 29 March 2016].

Bartels, L. (2010) 'Diversion programs for Indigenous women', *Research in Practice*, www.aic.gov.au/publications/current%20series/rip/1-10/13.html [Accessed 12 April 2016].

Belknap, J. (2001) *The Invisible Woman: Gender, Crime, and Justice*. London: Wadsworth.

Bloom, B. and Covington, S. (1998) 'Gender-specific programming for female offenders: what is it and why is it important?', paper presented at the 50th annual meeting of the American Society of Criminology, Washington, DC, November 11–14.

Bloom, B. and Covington, S. (1999) 'Gender-responsive programming and evaluation for females in the criminal justice system: a shift from What Works? to What is the Work?', paper presented at the 51st Annual Meeting of the American Society of Criminology, Toronto, ON, Canada, November 17–20.

Bloom, B., Owen, B. and Covington, S. (2003) *Gender-Responsive Strategies: Research, Practice and Guiding Principles for Women Offenders*. Washington, DC: U.S. Department of Justice, National Institute of Corrections.

Bonta, J. (1995) 'The responsivity principle and offender rehabilitation', *Forum on Corrections Research*, 7(3): 34–37.

Buell, M. (2015) 'Gender-responsive practices; where do we start?', *Corrections Today*, 77 (January/February): 16–18.

Calhoun, S., Messina, N., Cartier, J. and Torres, S. (2010) 'Implementing gender-responsive treatment for women in prison: client and staff perspectives', *Probation*, 74(3): 27–33.

Carlen, P. (2008) *Imaginary Penalities*. Cullompton: Willan.

Carloni, A.S. (1987) *Women in Development: A.I.D.'s Experience, 1973–1985. Vol. I.* Synthesis Paper. A.I.D. Program Evaluation Report No. 18.Washington, DC: U.S. Agency for International Development.

Carlton, B. and Segrave, M. (2015) 'Rethinking women's post-release reintegration and "success"', *Australian & New Zealand Journal of Criminology*, 49(2): 1–19.

Chesney-Lind, M. (1997) *The Female Offender: Girls, Women, and Crime*. Thousand Oaks, CA: Sage.

Chesney-Lind, M. and Okamoto, S. (2001) 'Gender matters: patterns in girls' delinquency and gender responsive programming', *Journal of Forensic Psychology Practice*, 1(3): 1–28.

Correctional Service of Canada (1990) *Creating Choices: The Report of the Task Force on Federally Sentenced Women*. Ottawa: Correctional Service of Canada, www.csc-scc.gc.ca/002/002/choice1e-eng.shtml [Accessed 29 March 2016].

Corston, J. (2007) *Women with Particular Vulnerabilities in the Criminal Justice System*. London: Home Office.

Covington, S. and Bloom, B. (2003) 'Gendered justice: women in the criminal justice system', in Bloom, B. (ed), *Gendered Justice: Addressing Female Offenders*. Durham, NC: Carolina Academic Press, pp. 3–23.

Covington, S. and Bloom, B. (2006) 'Gender responsive treatment and services in correctional settings', *Women and Therapy*, 29(3–4): 9–33.

Gardner, A. (2004) 'Spotlight on … the gender responsive unit', *Children's Legal Rights Journal*, 24(2): 51–52.

Gideon, L. (2011) 'Corrections in an era of reentry', in Gideon, L. (ed), *Rethinking Corrections: Rehabilitation, Reentry, and Reintegration*. Thousand Oaks, CA: Sage, pp. 1–18.

Hannah-Moffat, K. (1991) 'Creating choices or repeating history: Canadian female offenders and correctional reform', *Social Justice*, 18(3): 184–203.

Hannah-Moffat, K. (2002) 'Creating choices: reflecting on choices', in Carlen, P. (ed), *Women and Punishment: The Struggle for Justice*. Cullompton: Willan, pp. 199–219.

Hannah-Moffat, K. (2008) 'Re-imaging gendered penalties: the myth of gender-responsivity', in Carlen, P., *Imaginary Penalities*. Cullompton: Willan, pp. 193–217.

Harm Reduction International (2010) 'United Nations rules for the treatment of women prisoners and non-custodial measures for women offenders (the Bangkok Rules)', *Harm Reduction International Blog*, 4 November, www.ihra.net/contents/811 [Accessed 31 March 2016].

Hedderman, C. (2010) 'Government policy on women offenders: Labour's legacy and the coalition's challenge', *Punishment and Society*, 12(4): 485–500.

Hedderman, C., Palmer, E. and Hollin, C. (2008) 'Implementing services for women offenders and those "at risk" of offending: action research with "Together Women"', Ministry of Justice Research Series, 12/08. London: Ministry of Justice.

Holfreter, K. and Cupp, R. (2007) 'Gender and risk assessment: the empirical status of the LSI-R for women', *Journal of Contemporary Criminal Justice*, 23(4): 363–382.

Home Office (2004) *Women's Offending Reduction Programme: Action Plan*. London: Home Office.

Hubbard, D.J. and Matthews, B. (2008) 'Reconciling the differences between the "gender-responsive" and the "what works" literatures to improve services for girls', *Crime & Delinquency*, 54(2): 225–258.

Hughes, G. (2007) *The Politics of Crime and Community*. Basingstoke: Palgrave.

McIvor, G. (2004) *Women Who Offend*. London: Jessica Kingsley.

MacKinnon, C. (2011) 'Substantive equality: a perspective', *Minnesota Law Review*, 96(1): 1–27.

Messina, N., Grella, C.E., Cartier, J. and Torres, S. (2010) 'A randomized experimental study of gender-responsive substance abuse treatment for women in prison', *Journal of Substance Abuse Treatment*, 38(2): 97–107.

Miller-Ashton, J. (1993) 'Canada's new federal system for female offenders', in American Correctional Association, *Female Offender: Meeting the Needs of a Neglected Population*. Baltimore, MD: United Book Press, pp. 105–111.

Morgan, M. and Patton, P. (2002) 'Gender-responsive programming in the justice system – Oregon's guidelines for effective programming for girls', *Federal Probation*, 66(2): 57–65.

Prendergast, M.L., Messina, N., Hall, E.A. and Warda, U.S. (2011) 'The relative effectiveness of women-only and mixed-gender treatment for substance-abusing women', *Journal of Substance Abuse Treatment*, 40(4): 336–348.

Saksana, A. (2007) 'CEDAW: mandate for substantive equality', *Indian Journal of Gender Studies*, 14(3): 481–498.

Salime, Z. (2011) *Social Movements, Protest and Contention: Between Feminism and Islam. Human Rights and Sharia Law in Morocco*. Minneapolis: University of Minnesota Press.

Salisbury, E.J., Van Voorhis, P. and Spiropoulos, G.V. (2009) 'The predictive validity of a gender-responsive needs assessment: an exploratory study', *Crime and Delinquency*, 55(4): 550–585.

Scottish Executive (1998) *Women Offenders – A Safer Way – A Review of Community Disposals and the Use of Custody for Women Offenders in Scotland*. Edinburgh: The Stationery Office, Scotland.

Scottish Executive (2002) *A Better Way: The Report of the Ministerial Group on Women's Offending*. Edinburgh: Scottish Executive.

Stalans, L.J. (2009) 'Women's offending behavior: evidence-based review of gender differences and gender responsive programs', *Victims & Offenders: An International Journal of Evidence-based Research, Policy, and Practice*, 4(4): 405–411.

Steffensmeier, D., Schwartz, J., Zhong, H. and Ackerman, J. (2005) 'An assessment of recent trends in girls' violence using diverse longitudinal sources: is the gender gap closing?', *Criminology*, 43(2): 355–406.

UN (2001a) 'Beijing Declaration and Platform for Action', www.un.org/womenwatch/daw/beijing/pdf/BDPfA%20E.pdf [Accessed 16 March 2016].

UN (2001b) 'Supporting gender mainstreaming', Office of the Special Adviser on Gender Issues and Advancement of Women, United Nations, www.un.org/womenwatch/osagi/pdf/report.pdf [Accessed 28 July 2016].

UN (2009a) 'Overview of the Convention', UN Women, www.un.org/womenwatch/daw/cedaw/ [Accessed 30 March 2016].

UN (2009b) 'Short history of CEDAW Convention', UN Women, www.un.org/womenwatch/daw/cedaw/history [Accessed 30 March 2016].

UN (2010) *United Nations Rules for the Treatment of Women Prisoners and Non-Custodial Measures for Women Offenders (the Bangkok Rules)*. UN General Assembly.

Van Voorhis, P. and Presser, L. (2001) *Classification of Women Offenders: A National Assessment of Current Practices*. Washington, DC: US Department of Justice, National Institute of Corrections.

Van Wormer, K. (2010) *Working with Female Offenders: A Gender-Sensitive Approach*. Hoboken, NJ: John Wiley and Sons.

Worral, A. and Gelsthorpe, L. (2009) '"What works" with women offenders: the past 30 years', *Probation Journal*, 56(4): 329–345.

Chapter 4

Gender responsivity and the male gaze

The argument for gender-responsive justice has, in the main, addressed itself to the 'problem' of women and their treatment at the hands of criminal justice agencies. As Connell recounts, this focus on females rather than males is true of gender politics more generally which were developed as a consequence of concerns developed around the gendered injustices faced by the female sex. She remarks:

> It is hardly surprising that the issue of gender equality was placed on the policy agenda by women. The reason is obvious: it is women who are disadvantaged by the main patterns of gender inequality and who therefore have the claim for redress.
>
> (Connell 2005:1802)

However, in more recent years, as the call for gender-responsive justice has begun to be heard there have been calls to explore gender as an issue for men and boys too. This chapter will look at the evolution of this idea explaining in more detail the female-focus of the debate and considering the different arguments which have been put forward which support, or reject, the call for an expansion of gender-responsive justice so that it incorporates the experiences of men and boys too.

Feminism and the problem of men

The debate around gender-responsive justice has been largely fought and advanced within the terrain of feminist politics. As we have seen, the argument was forged in the struggles of the second wave of feminism which emerged as a force in the late 1970s and early 1980s. This late-twentieth-century feminism was influenced by a number of social movements and famously 'fragmented' (Rowbotham, Segal and Wainwright 1979) into multiple perspectives, all with the endpoint of achieving equality for women but with different understandings of the root of that oppression and therefore adopting different strategies to realise gender equality. One of the key early 'splits' which is pertinent to this chapter was between 'radical' and 'socialist' feminisms, which adopted different perspectives on the part which men could play in furthering the aims of the women's movement. To pare this argument down to its most essential elements, radical feminism perceived the oppression of women as rooted in the power of the male body and its use as a tool of violent domination over women while socialist feminists saw the oppression of women as arising from the organisation of class society, which under capitalism had taken a particular and specific form, restricting women's access to the labour market, trapping them in domesticity or low-paid work and ensuring their status in society as dependent on and serving the needs of men (Sargent and Hartmann 1986).

The disparate standpoints of socialist and radical feminists were brought together in the dual systems theory developed by Heidi Hartmann (1979). Hartmann argued that the sex/gender system of patriarchy and the economic system of capitalism were so interlinked as to have formed a single entity, patriarchal capitalism, which was responsible for the multifaceted and many-layered experience of women's oppression. Both systems, Hartmann argued, were mutually reinforcing with men's power over women overshadowing all other experiences and limiting women's capacity to live outside of the boundaries set by dominant social stereotypes as to what constitutes the 'good woman'. In turn women's labour is devalued under capitalism, performing caring and domestic responsibilities become an expectation of the good woman and this labour is given freely to family and friends or paid poorly when performed within the labour market (Walby 1988). Patriarchy thereby directly benefits capitalism, providing an ongoing source of cheap labour while it also presents obvious advantages to individual males who have their own and their family's needs met by the women in their life at little or no cost. As an additional bonus for the male sex, women's dependence on men for financial security ensures that women are taught to perform their gender in a way which is considered will attract men to them in order that they may gain the security otherwise denied to them as a single female. Women and girls are thereby trained to adopt a subservient role within their relationships with men and boys, to service the needs of the men in their life in order, once attracted, to keep them by performing the dominant tropes of femininity, of passivity and of sexual display. As a consequence all women and girls occupy a particularly vulnerable position in society, one in which their well-being and self-esteem are placed in the hands of men who subsequently gain the advantage in both their public and private relationships to the female sex.

The idea that men benefit from the oppression of women has significant implications for the struggle for gender justice. If the cause of women's oppression is rooted in men's dominance, both physically and psychically in a sex-gender system which sustains systems of patriarchal control, then to escape that oppression women must work together to build alternative structures which are women-centred, designed by women for women. Men have no role to play in this process but they must nevertheless eventually be persuaded to give up the advantages bestowed on them by virtue of their sex if gender justice is ever to be attained. Socialist feminists, on the other hand, suggest that the interests of the male sex ultimately coincide with the emancipation of women and therefore this feminist standpoint will grant more of a role to men and boys in collaborating with the female sex to combat women's oppression. Segal, for example, while acknowledging the 'extraordinary difficulty of confronting men's cultural and social dominance' (Segal 1989:14) within progressive social movements as well as within a more conservative politics, nevertheless praises the focus of the early women's liberation movement which called on women to enter those institutions which had previously been bastions of male privilege and by doing so, to transform them. The early women's movement in the UK, for example, put great store on women becoming active in trade unions as a key strategy in highlighting issues of concern to women nationally and in winning concessions in the workplace which would improve women's pay and conditions of work, allowing women to achieve the financial security they needed but also demonstrating that women's issues were men's issues too. She uses the example of the 'historic' trade union march for abortion rights[1] which took place in London in 1979 as a significant moment in winning what had been a predominantly masculinist and male-centred institution over to the consideration of issues which had previously been considered and marginalised as 'women's issues'.

There has been a continued and fierce debate within feminism as to the part which men can play in women's liberation. What all standpoints within feminism acknowledge, however, is that the privilege and authority which have been bestowed on men over many centuries and which have become engrained and enmeshed in all aspects of day-to-day culture and in the deepest structures of society will not be overturned without tremendous difficulty and that men will not give up their power simply on request. However, as Connell (2005:1809–1810) reveals, the role of men and boys in promoting gender equality 'emerged as a significant issue in international discussions in the 1990s' as the Fourth World Conference on Women, held in Beijing in 1995, first raised the issue in a transnational arena of men's responsibility in promoting equality. The issue was raised again in the UN General Assembly in 2000, as the subject of an online seminar hosted by the UN in 2003 and again as a major theme for the UN Commission on the Status of Women in 2004.

The study of men and masculinities

Feminist insights and theory have generated a great deal of discussion around the nature of the male sex and of the impact of masculinist discourses and behaviours on female experience. Indeed, feminism has inspired a new academic discipline based around the study of men and later of masculinity. This new area of study emerged in the 1980s within what Connell and others term 'the metropole' in response to feminism's problematisation of the male and the misogynistic and sexist attitudes which were seen to pervade male culture in the West. Rather than problematising and casting females as the object of study and as the 'outliers' of society, this new discipline placed men and boys under critical scrutiny for the first time. The theories which emerged were largely sociological in nature. They rejected biological explanations for male behaviour but also looked further than simplistic 'sex-role' theories which had previously located perceived differences in male and female behaviour in the different social roles ascribed to each sex; hence the male was ascribed as the outward-facing protector and breadwinner, the female as the family-oriented carer and home-maker and their behaviours and attitudes reflected this material reality. Instead the new investigation of the male sex emphasised the more deeply embedded and cultural manifestations of male power and hegemony, taking its cue from post-structuralist approaches which emphasised the construction of masculinity within Western societies and the discourses which supported and sustained the idealisation of the metropolitan male, the normalisation of masculinity and the subordination of the female and of femininity (Connell 2014).

Feminist praxis challenged men to confront their behaviour and to find ways in which men could support the feminist goal of achieving equality for women. This challenge carried within it the idea that men could resist gender inequalities and could change their behaviour if they were won to the feminist project. As feminism created the concept of consciousness-raising for women, so men were encouraged to form men's groups, to examine their own assumptions and understandings as to what was considered 'normal' male cognition and action. So the idea of the 'new man', the (subsequently much-parodied) anti-violence, pro-woman, domesticated and family-involved anti-sexist male, was born. Some men, within academia, took up the challenge set by their feminist colleagues and began to investigate normative constructions of the male body and psyche. As their study shifted towards the study of masculinity rather than merely the male, the study of men took on a new dynamic and focus. Men were not merely the sum of their actions (as understood within sex-role theory), which could be altered once consciousness of their oppressive practices was understood and acknowledged, but carried in their embodiment a range of social expectations which were deeply embedded within the culture and psyche of society as a whole. In addition, sex-role theory was found insufficiently able to account for significant power differentials between men and women and additionally between men from different social backgrounds. It became clear that to change cultural expectations and relations of power would involve more than a change in the practices of individual men, rather a much bigger social and cultural shift would be required – one which would involve the deconstruction of masculinity and which would challenge its acceptance by men and by women too.

The new emphasis on the men as a focus of study widened the field of gender studies to incorporate the importance of gender as a central feature shaping men's lives too. Prior to this break, men had been treated as though they had no gender and as though that which was applicable to the male could be universally applied (Kimmel and Messner 2010). This shift in emphasis was significant therefore in challenging the view of male behaviour as the norm to which all, including females, should aspire and in helping to raise awareness that *formal equality*, and sameness of treatment, meant shoehorning females into systems and institutions which were built for and by men. All this had been concealed from view as centuries of scientific, economic, political and social theory had rested on the assumption that how men saw the world was the way that the world was constructed. Men's studies were suggested as a tool through which these long-held assumptions could be subjected to close examination.

Hegemonic masculinity and emphasised femininity

One of the most enduring and much-used conceptual tools which has been embraced within the broad church which developed around studies of males and masculinity has been the concept of 'hegemonic masculinity' which surfaced in an Australian study by Kessler and others in 1982 (Connell and Messerschmidt 2005). It was further explored by Connell in a number of publications published in the early 1980s and refined in her 1987 book *Gender and Power*. The concept of hegemonic masculinity was formulated through a combination of insights from feminist theories of patriarchy, a Gramscian understanding of class relations and cultural change, critical role-theory, the concept of subordinated masculinities developed within the movement for gay liberation, empirical research on local cultures of masculinity and insights from the field of psychoanalysis which demonstrated that there were significant tensions and contradictions within the normal operation of conventional masculinity (Connell and Messerschmidt 2005:831–832). The introduction and subsequent widespread adoption of this concept further underlined the variability in men's experiences, replacing the concept of masculinity with its plural form, masculinities. Studies of masculinities revealed that many men experienced forms of violence and prejudice from other males, but also demonstrated that although hegemonic masculinity can only be achieved by a minority of men it 'required all other men to position themselves in relation to it' and by doing so 'it ideologically legitimated the global subordination of women to men' (Connell and Messerschmidt 2005:832). The acceptance of a hegemonic masculinity assured males power over women in all their relationships – social, economic and sexual. The idealisation of hegemonic masculinity permeated the institutional and cultural frameworks of society as well as intimate and personal relationships. It was inescapable, overarching and ensured that dominant forms of masculinity prevailed and that other gendered practices were subordinated to it and subject to social censure.

The shift from studies of men to studies of masculinity held certain promises for the achievement of gender equality but also highlighted significant barriers. Connell and others stressed the changing nature of hegemonic masculinity historically as well as its contemporary local manifestations. While the global reach of the concept demonstrated the power of metropolitan formations of masculinity around the world, research in different regions of the globe revealed that local cultures of masculinity could be differently manifested. Historical research too proved that hegemonic masculinity had taken different forms in past periods, all of which held out the hope that masculinity could change in the future. However, at the same time hegemonic masculinity, whatever its local manifestation, appears to have always incorporated the central idea of male power and dominance over the female sex. Hegemonic masculinity, it has been argued, reflects rather than creates differential power structures and the focus on masculinity obscures the realities of gendered power which are far more engrained than the concept can acknowledge. Masculinity studies have also been criticised for not dealing adequately with the issue of male violence against women or taking on an explicitly feminist framework and perspective (McCarry 2007).

Connell's work on developing the concept of hegemonic masculinity clearly positioned masculinity as relational, in that masculinity only makes sense as a concept when understood as a counterpoint to femininity. While Connell's work on hegemonic masculinity has been much cited there has been less attention paid to the important complement of hegemonic masculinity, that of 'emphasised femininity' which exists alongside and is accepting of ideas of hegemonic masculinity (Connell 1987). As such it is constituted as a femininity which is based on women accepting their subordinate role and supporting and thereby reinforcing hegemonic masculinity. Both hegemonic masculinity and emphasised femininity are constituted by social practices and positions which men and women can adopt individually but which are collectively legitimated. Emphasised femininity is expressed in conformity to an idealised version of femininity and culturally acceptable idealisations of the desirable female. It also encompasses a position of heterosexuality and the goal of attracting a suitable, male, life-partner who will adopt the stereotypical male qualities of breadwinner and protector. Emphasised femininity cannot, and does not set out to, challenge the idea that males are the superior sex and is based on an acceptance of existing power relations. It confers on those women who adopt it a form of cultural or sexual capital. It can be utilised in many ways, embodied and expressed through particular styles of clothing and demeanour, and in different spaces, used in the boardroom as well as the bedroom to confer certain advantages to the female adopter (Mattsson 2015). Due to its social dominance the expression of emphasised femininity is considered as natural by many rather than as socially constituted. As men can feel more comfortable and powerful as they achieve a closer relationship to hegemonic masculinity, so women's self-esteem and confidence can increase the nearer they come to achieving the embodiment and performance of the idealised and typical female. For these reasons women and girls can feel that this accomplishment brings them a level of power, autonomy and choice which might otherwise be lacking in their lives (Skeggs 1997).

Alongside the physical embodiment of emphasised femininity is the injunction for women to develop other attributes and especially to become a supportive, empathetic and caring creature. Again these qualities can assist the female to access the labour market in certain roles such as nursing or education which are largely considered as suited to women's innate abilities. These attributed qualities are also key to women's treatment within the criminal justice system. Women and girls are perceived very differently depending on the crimes for which they are charged. There is ample evidence, for example, which demonstrates that women who commit 'masculine' crimes (serious and violent offences such as homicide, sexual assault or robbery) are treated disproportionately more harshly than women who commit 'feminine' (misdemeanour or non-violent) crimes. This is an observation which has been made many times but as late as 2014 research again revealed that women convicted of 'masculine crimes' in the New Zealand courts are still more likely to be sentenced to longer custodial sentences than males who had been similarly convicted and that this mirrors the double-standard which has been persistently applied in courts in many other regions of the world (Mann, Menih and Smith 2014:358). Conversely, the closer any female conforms to idealised gender stereotypes then the more lenient the courts will tend to be. Those females who are seen to perform their caring responsibilities well, to be passive, meek and submissive to the authorities, are afforded greater leeway. Females are therefore further trained into adopting submissive attitudes, dressing to complement feminine expectations and to conform to their socially proscribed gender roles as the 'good' and 'respectable' woman (Kruttschnitt 1982). The consequences of failing to meet these expectations can be severe and as a consequence women and girls are further silenced, unable to express anger or frustration and to justify what they might consider as righteous anger or violent reactions to their own victimisation. 'Emphasized femininity' strips women of their agency, of their voices and of the right to fight back against harms committed against them.

Feminism, anti-feminism and the study of men

Those studies of men which emerged in the 1970s and early 1980s were, not surprisingly, heavily influenced by feminist theory (Kimmel and Messner 2010:xv). These studies explored ways in which tradition and the construction of gendered norms affected men's relationship to themselves and others, arguing that alongside the power which is bestowed on men and boys as a consequence of their sex, the gendered expectations which come with possessing a male body can also have negative effects on men's relationship to themselves and to others. These studies saw dominant forms of masculinity as problematic and emphasised the powerful constraints which these constructions of masculinity place on male behaviour, demanding the creation of tough, aggressive and misogynistic male personas who are expected to stand on their own two feet, hide their emotional responses and bury any sign of weakness. These 'attributes' are instilled into boys through social, familial and peer pressures which are often manifest through teasing, humiliation and violence towards others (Kivel 1999). It is unsurprising then that boys learn to apply such techniques to control others and that they can bring these expectations and behaviours into their most intimate relationships. Such problematic constructions of masculinity have been used to explain the disproportionate use of violence by the male sex. Kimmel and Messner (2010) invite us to:

> Take a look at the numbers: Men constitute 99 percent of all persons arrested for rape, 88 percent of those arrested for murder, 92 percent of those arrested for robbery, 87 percent for aggravated assault, 85 percent of other assaults, 83 percent of all family violence, and 82 percent of disorderly conduct. Nearly 90 percent of all murder victims are killed by men.
>
> (533)

Yet, as Kimmel and Messner go on to observe, the daily litany of violence meted out by men and reported by the media as a series of newsworthy events is never presented as a general social problem associated with maleness or masculinity. However, as soon as a suicide bomber, murderer or violent gang member is discovered to be female, then the sex of the perpetrator elicits immediate attention and there is much speculation as to whether, as a consequence of female criminality, society is breaking down and becoming more violent. The facts of male violence are so engrained in our general understanding of the way that human relations across the globe are constituted, that there is no media story here and nothing which would raise any necessity to further comment. While the violent and harmful acts which men engage in are themselves subject to media attention, the fact that they are committed so overwhelmingly by men and boys largely passes society by. In the same way the day-to-day objectification and denigration of women and girls, which are also part of the training of men, are so overwhelmingly accepted that they are rarely challenged or even attended to unless they are considered to have crossed a barrier of acceptability or negatively impacted on someone who is already in the public eye and thereby already of interest to the media. For those of us who are unknown and therefore unimportant in the eyes of the media, our humiliation and victimisation go unremarked and we remain largely unprotected.

The raising of issues connected with the personal safety of females by the women's movement in the 1970s was an important aspect of the impact of feminism. Feminist theorists and activists forced the twin issues of violence against women and women's fears towards men into the public agenda for the first time (Stanko 1992). This was a revolutionary moment for women. Matters of concern to women and girls were raised as universal problems which should be addressed by society more generally. The raising of these issues meant that a new vocabulary was developed which allowed problems which had been unaddressed, experiences which had been untold and grievances which had been unaired to be spoken (Cain 1990). Women could subsequently better articulate their feelings, reveal how certain male behaviour made them uncomfortable and openly call out and challenge men's sexism. As the studies of men at this time reveal, feminism opened up the arena within which men could also begin to question their own behaviours, to try to understand from where they were forged and to attempt to change themselves and others. The violence of men was subject to some scrutiny, although as some have argued, while a clearer acknowledgement of the extent and range of men's violence did develop, the violence has not diminished as a result and is still poorly understood (McCarry 2007:404).

There is some evidence that feminist arguments have been embraced by men's groups working actively to counter male hegemony in society. Masculinity scholars have pointed to the growth of groups and networks of men who have come together across the globe to support women in their fight for equality. Flood (2005:458–459) considers anti-violence activism by men as the most well-developed and persistent of such endeavours but they also include groups of men who are concerned to develop greater connection with their children or to offer more egalitarian familial relationships. There are many others who have spoken out against the objectification and commodification of women and girls or actively promoted equality in various ways by working in alliance with women (Connell 2005:1809–1810). These campaigning groups demonstrate that 'men can be and are motivated by interests other than those of gender privilege' (Flood 2005:459). They must, however, as Flood argues, be wary of inadvertently reinforcing their privileged position as they come to the struggle with a favoured status and should be ready to listen to women at all times and to relinquish power and advantage where this is felt to be necessary.

The early connection between the study of men and its roots in feminism has not been universally sustained. Starting in the US a split has developed in the discipline between a largely uncritical 'Men's Studies' and the more radical 'Critical Studies of Men' which still retains its connection with feminist theory (McCarry 2007). According to Robinson (2003) the more conservative 'Men's Studies' has triumphed over a more critical engagement with masculinity in a number of academic departments and has succeeded in taking resources away from feminist-inspired 'Women's Studies'. The theory which emanates from these 'Men's Studies' departments, Robinson argues, makes only a token reference to feminism and then often distorts the theory and practice of the women's movement, cherry-picking feminist theory which can be used to support their work but misrepresenting or ignoring that which does not. Outside of academia too, a 'men's movement' has emerged which has little to do with lessons which feminist activism brought to more general attention and which on the contrary is based, to a great extent, on the repudiation of much which is associated with feminism. These 'men's rights' groups have taken the position that males now represent the sex which is most disadvantaged in a society which privileges women in domestic and parental relationships. They have formed to organise for changes in family law which they now consider to be gender-biased in favour of the female sex. Self-styled 'father's rights' groups such as 'Fathers4Justice' and 'Families Need Fathers' have mobilised activists in countries such as the US and the UK where divorce and separation rates are highest and around the claim that the court system favours maternal over paternal rights. They have organised a number of high-profile activist 'stunts' which have seen individual males, who feel that they have been denied what they consider sufficient access to their children, involved in climbing buildings and staging banner-drops to publicise their claims. Such groups are generally considered to be anti-feminist and misogynist by those who have carried out research into their activities and standpoint (Flood 2005). While these men's rights groups have grown in number and in public recognition over the last two decades, Flood's research shows that their activism is often sporadic and individual membership is often short-lived. More worrying is the growth of a more general anti-feminist backlash which has seen a reassertion of men's rights in a much more sustained manner and which is further discussed later.

Whatever happened to patriarchy?

Somewhere along the line the term 'patriarchy' used by early feminists to explain the dominant power relations of men over women was dropped and gender equality/inequality became the preferred terms in use (Holter 2005:17). This loss of the term in much academic literature coincided with the introduction of men's studies into the university departments and the adoption of a model which recognised differential power relations within the male experience and the existence of multiple masculinities (Carrigan, Connell and Lee 1985). According to this view male power could not be said to be universally applied. Some men held power over others, both male and female, while other males lacked power and were subordinated to other males. Once women began to gain opportunities to hold political and economic power it was argued that patriarchy was dissolving and that some women, for example those who had attained management positions, now held power over men. For more critical theorists this apparent disappearance of patriarchy always presented problems – patriarchy, as with many power structures, they argued, is hidden and obscured from view so may have just taken a different form. So while it was apparent that women and girls were making great strides forward in breaking through existing barriers to personal achievement and creating new opportunities for the female sex, the underlying social structures which still ensured all women, whatever their status, were subject to male power remained firmly in place. As Holter (2005) explains:

> Many operative patriarchal structures are difficult to perceive directly, although we witness their effects. Sometimes the tracks disappear. Examples include wage-work restructuring that devalues women and social competence and labor market regulations that work to the same effect ... Conversely, in areas where the effects of patriarchy seem fairly visible, such as with the persistent social problems of rape or battering, it is not so easy to tell the societal and cultural causes and the effects on society in general.
>
> (19–20)

For Holter, patriarchy involves the systematic oppression of women which is also inherently linked to the subordination of non-privileged males. Such males are held with contempt because they are more closely linked with the feminine and their masculinity is thereby questioned. Patriarchal relations of power can just as easily be turned in this manner against other males. Nevertheless this does not strip the subordinated of their recourse to patriarchal privilege and all males, whether from dominant or subordinate groups, can use the power of their sex to intimidate and control women and girls. Women and girls, however, do not have access to patriarchal power. They may gain access to other privileges and the power which is associated with these, through their class position or their ascribed racial status, for example, but they are still rendered vulnerable as females in a heavily patriarchal world.

Outside the realms of critical theory, however, gender relations appear to have been greatly altered over the last few decades, at least in those regions of the world where feminist activism has succeeded in opening up the spaces in which women are considered as legitimate contributors. So in these areas the term patriarchy has been generally dropped in favour of use of the term gender inequality and as a consequence the illusion is sown of there being a much more level playing field between the sexes. Gender inequality does not encompass the idea of a generalised power and dominance of the male sex but instead suggests that gender inequality can be measured and compared across different social situations. A workforce contains 50 per cent women who are paid equally to men? Then gender equality has been achieved. Legislation is changed to allow women to hold bank accounts, mortgages and companies in their own names? Then this stands as another example of gender equality. Furthermore, such a measurement of the attainment of equality can quite easily be used to argue that men are now the victims. Female students are achieving better results at school and winning more places at university? Then boys are now experiencing a detriment because the educational curriculum has become too feminised. An individual man is denied custody of his children after the break-up of a relationship? Then this is held as an example of where social structures of gender work in favour of the female and show males as lacking in power.

The gender equality perspective is apparent in the work of transnational organisations working to improve conditions for women. When organisations working in development first acknowledged the importance of gender in the late 1970s and early 1980s their focus was very much women-centred. The policy agenda of 'women in development' concentrated its activities on the involvement of women in the implementation of policies which were considered as central to the transformation of underdeveloped societies. By the later years of the 1980s, however, this approach was considered as flawed in that it 'focused in a simplistic way on a set of agents (women) and ignored the context of relationships and power relations in which these women operated' (Morrell and Swart 2005:100). In other words women could not be separated from the gendered power relations into which they were entrapped. The solution incorporated the use of a new designation 'gender and development', an approach which was designed to move away from one which saw men as obstacles to gender equality but to understand the gendered cultural context in which relations between men and women operated and to try to develop a common understanding and a way forward which incorporated men in the process of change, although women still remained the primary focus. From the mid-1990s however, and publicly articulated in the Beijing Declaration adopted by the Fourth World Conference on Women in 1995, the UN adopted a policy stance which was considered more inclusive, arguing that both women and men had to share equally in the responsibility of working to end discrimination against women. The strategy of *gender mainstreaming*, enshrined in policy subsequent to the Beijing conference, demonstrates this turn to include men's experiences in future policy deliberations. Gender mainstreaming was designed to put consideration of gender equality impacts at the heart of all decision-making and it became clear that men should not be disadvantaged as a consequence. A report emanating from the UN Office of the Special Adviser on Gender Issues and Advancement of Women clarifies this point. It explains gender mainstreaming as:

> the process of assessing the implications for women and men of any planned action, including legislation, policies or programmes, in all areas and at all levels. It is a strategy for making women's as well as men's concerns and experiences an integral dimension of the design, implementation, monitoring and evaluation of policies and programmes in all political, economic and societal spheres so that women and men benefit equally and inequality is not perpetuated. The ultimate goal is to achieve gender equality.
>
> (UN 2001)

The shift from a woman-centred to a gender-centred approach has continued to dominate development agendas. A report written to the Expert Group

Meeting on 'The role of men and boys in achieving gender equality' in 2003 set out the policy terms written up by CEDAW on the subject of men and boys:

> governments expressed their determination to encourage men to participate fully in all actions towards gender equality. The Declaration emphasized that equal sharing of responsibilities and a harmonious partnership between women and men were critical to their well-being and that of their families as well as to the consolidation of democracy. The Platform for Action emphasized the principle of shared power and responsibility between women and men at home, in the workplace and in the wider national and international communities. It stressed that gender equality could only be achieved when men and women worked together in partnerships, and that the principle of equality of women and men had to be integral to the socialization process. Specific actions aim in particular at promoting harmonization of work and family responsibilities for men and women; at encouraging men to share equally in child care and household work; and at promoting programmes to educate and enable men to assume their responsibilities to prevent HIV/AIDS and other sexually transmitted diseases (STDs).
>
> (Marinova 2003)

Later documents began to consider women's rights from the perspective of human rights but also to include the argument that men and boys were also subject to harmful practices which were based in the same patriarchal traditions which treated women and girls in such a discriminatory manner and to argue that they would also greatly benefit from these practices' elimination (UN 2014).

This move to involve men in the struggle for gender equality did not go unremarked and without criticism. It has been seen as re-establishing a perspective which places men's needs at the centre and therefore as a return to the bad old days when all development strategies were directed towards men and masculinist in tone. The critics of this new approach argue that just at the point at which women were being placed centre-stage, this new perspective derailed much of the progress which had been made and placed women firmly back into the margins (Morrell and Swart 2005). Previous approaches which had positively discriminated in favour of women had retained a harder political edge, more closely associated with critical feminist approaches which started with the need to put right centuries of discrimination and harm which had been meted out to the female sex as a direct result of patriarchal power structures. They stood in a more revolutionary and radical tradition which set out to overthrow existing structures of power and to demand rights for women which would require the dismantling of male privileges. More recent gender-centred approaches are more liberal in their analysis – they argue that reforms can be attained within current conditions and that men can be won over to new ideals of masculinity without the need for fundamental societal change.

Gender symmetry and the anti-feminist backlash

It is undoubtedly true that men and boys are also caught up in the web of social constructions of gender and can be negatively impacted as a consequence. Social constructions of masculinity force men and boys into particular moulds which can be uncomfortable and harmful to the bearer. The internationally renowned British artist Grayson Perry has described masculinity as a callous and brittle carapace which is strong, yet inflexible and which can be easily shattered, leaving some men in difficult and more vulnerable positions. He notes that masculinity is worn by many as a protective shield but that 'the weight of the armour becomes a burden [to men]' so that everyday performance of masculinity can easily lead men to reify aggression and violence to such an extent that this can take centre-stage in their lives (Channel 4 2016). In addition men are called upon to provide defence and protection of nation and of family and to prepare themselves physically and mentally for such tasks and this presents them with a heavy burden. Perry's assessment of masculinity and its impacts is clearly sympathetic to the plight of the male in Western society. As a cross-dresser who wears his masculinity more lightly than many men, Perry is in a good position to interrogate the harmful effects which gendered stereotypes can have on men and boys and to throw much needed light on this significant subject. Remaining cognisant of and understanding these harmful effects, however, does not require a rejection of the idea that society is profoundly shaped by patriarchal structures of power and that women and girls are disproportionately disadvantaged in all areas of their lives as a consequence.

The disproportionate disadvantaging of the female experience under patriarchy does not mean that males cannot and do not feel pain too as a consequence of this (dis)ordering of society. However, it is important to note that there is not an equivalence in the harms done to males and females under patriarchy. The harms done to women are of a different order and magnitude. Patriarchy privileges the male sex in society and creates systems whereby the female sex is denied access to privilege based on their ascribed biological sex, a sex which is considered to be inferior. It would be wrong to conflate the very real pains which masculinity can inflict on the individual male with the systematic destruction of privilege and creation of disadvantage which patriarchy confers on females as an entire social group. However, this conflation is attempted and has gained some considerable successes in turning concern and attention away from a woman-centred perspective which recognises the need to counter systemic discrimination against women. As Dragiewicz (2011) has cogently argued, the formation of men's rights groups in many parts of the industrialised West has reflected this shift in attention and concern. Concern is now expressed that men are the ultimate losers when women gain advantages, as though the fight for gender equality were some zero-sum game which necessarily and always means a step forward for women can only be achieved at men's expense. Consequently an anti-feminist backlash (Faludi 1991) has gained significant momentum in recent decades and has been successful in pulling back and even reversing many of the gains made by the women's movement, especially where these gains most directly affect women's relationship to men in intimate partnerships and domestic settings.

Since the resurgence of the movement for women's rights in the second half of the twentieth century, so much has changed for women that it is often said that women's equality has now been assured. The new social and economic circumstances in which men and women coexist represent a change in the manner in which patriarchy is played out in society but should not be taken as proof that patriarchy itself has been overthrown. As Walby (1990) has recognised, the social relations of patriarchy have never been fixed and unmoving and have altered over the centuries to accommodate the material conditions of existence in different societies and have adapted to changing social attitudes and economic structures. Despite alterations in the framing of relationships between the sexes however, and significant cultural shifts which have redrawn key social boundaries, the fundamental power imbalances which are so deeply enshrined in male-dominated and patriarchal societies continue to persist. It is galling therefore to witness the ascendancy of positions on gender which claim that society must step away from positively supporting women's causes and adopt, once more, a gender-blind or gender-neutral discourse and practice. As Dragiewicz (2011) has recorded in some detail, the consequences of this position have had serious implications for the maintenance of gender-specific services for women, most notably resulting in the withdrawal of state funding for all kinds of support for women fleeing violent relationships in different regions across North America. Indeed, the organisation of men against the gains of feminism has focused its attention on two key areas which feminism was able to successfully highlight as central to women's oppression – gendered violence and the family. In these areas women still remain highly vulnerable even after 50 and more years of struggle since the movement for women's rights re-emerged in the middle of the twentieth century (Dragiewicz and Mann 2016).

The anti-feminist and often openly misogynistic arguments which have been asserted by men's rights groups have gained more generalised social currency. An anti-progressive politics has gained increasing support across many regions of the globe since the turn of the current century and represents a danger to women's rights which are by no means firmly secured. Feminist arguments have been undermined and have been replaced by a presentation of ideas which reformulate problems such as those of intimate partner violence as unrelated to either gendered social relations or even the biological sex of the perpetrator. While flying in the face of all available data and interpretations of the available statistics which continue to demonstrate that the majority of violence in all societies is perpetrated by males and that a disproportionate amount of violence is male on female, the claim is made as to the symmetry of violence between the sexes. This claim to *gender symmetry* has been used to argue that the funding of projects which are gender-specific actually represents a violence towards males and a discrimination which needs to be outlawed (Dragiewicz 2011).

It is in this context of anti-feminist and backlash politics that the argument for the provision of gender-specific services must be placed. The persistence and continued emergence of new gender-specific practices must be credited to those feminist scholars and practitioners who have kept their particular vision alive. Nevertheless the ideas of gender symmetry and of the displacement of men's rights have crept into the conversation around gender-specific provision in quite subtle ways and given rise to suggestions that men's needs might also be served by gender-specific provision. This call can be interpreted in two ways – as a concern that the problem of masculinity must be addressed directly with men and as therefore learning once again from the insights of feminism, or it could be presented as a fundamental attack on the concept of gender-specific services for women and a rowing back on the gains which have been made over recent years. It is to this debate which we now turn.

Gender-responsivity and the problem of masculinity

To date there has been very little published on the topic of gender-specific services for men who break the law. In the main this lack of attention to the subject is a consequence of the backstory to the development of gender-specific services, which, as has been recounted, arose as a response to the harmful effects of shoehorning women and girls into a criminal justice system which was built to accommodate men. In effect therefore the criminal justice system, the courts, prisons and treatment programmes were already gender-specific and masculinist in their design but masquerading as gender-neutral. The male-centred nature of provision was rarely made obvious, there were few laws or practices which specified and required different treatment for females and as a consequence the fight for gender equality within the criminal justice system was not fought on the grounds of repealing discriminatory laws such as existed for example in the legislation surrounding labour laws which did actively bar women from certain occupations and withhold equal pay (Cunningham-Parmeter 2014). Instead those feminists concerned with the fair and equal punishment of women had to expose the myth of gender-neutrality in punishment regimes, to dismantle male-centred provision and to argue for a redesign and reformulation of systems in order to cater for the specific needs of women which had been long ignored. As systems of punishment had been assumed to be universally applicable, sameness in treatment was the status quo and it was this status quo which had to be challenged. From the start therefore the fight for equality in the criminal justice system was concerned with establishing sameness of treatment where gender discrimination could be exposed but in the main part it was focused around the need to acknowledge and work with difference between the sexes.

Feminism has been divided as to whether the struggle for women's rights would be best taken forward through highlighting the similarities between men and women or through highlighting women's distinct experiences. Those taking the equity standpoint that women should share equally in the rights and privileges which are afforded to men have argued that to extend rights to women based on their special circumstances, for example the experiences of pregnancy and menstruation which are not shared by men, would actually open the floodgates to further discrimination and give succour to those who take the position that women are biologically burdened, weaker than men and more vulnerable. This accommodation to women as a special case would in turn reinforce the view that females are in need of male protection and special consideration – which in reality would mean males adopting more patriarchal and controlling behaviour vis-a-vis the female sex in general. Those feminists opting for formal equality as the way forward have in addition adopted a liberal stance suggesting that equality can be achieved through legislative frameworks which outlaw discrimination and which afford both sexes the same rights and privileges. Those feminists adopting the substantive standpoint – that the different circumstances of women require different treatment to achieve equality in outcome – have highlighted the persistent nature of women's disadvantage which endures despite the repeal of discriminatory legislation and the enactment of laws which have put equal treatment on the agenda. They have instead taken the position that there is a need to work to reverse the harms of socialised gender-based differences which cannot be removed through legislation alone. In effect then this was an argument for positive discrimination, recognising the part which affirmative action could play in righting historical wrongs.

Those who have advocated for gender-specific services for men have often left it unclear as to on which side of the debate their own views fall. It is clear where the anti-feminist backlash groups are politically and philosophically situated. These groups contend that positive discrimination is in itself socially harmful and divisive. They base their assessments of such affirmative action on a sex-based rather than a gender-based analysis. In the eyes of the men's rights groups, equal treatment requires a challenge to any privileges which women have gained, on the grounds that these discriminate against the male sex. Theirs is a stand against substantive equality and is a denial of gender-based privilege and institutionalised masculinism which fall to the advantage of men and boys. More difficult to ascertain, however, are the underlying conceptual frameworks which lie behind support for and the promotion of gender-based treatment of boys and men made by pro-women advocates of gender-responsive justice. The sagacity of this position is often taken for granted by its proponents and has been introduced as an aside rather than as a fully articulated position. Van Wormer, for example, when describing the parameters of gender-sensitive treatment for women, adds:

> Gender-sensitive treatment can of course be oriented toward males to help them work on issues related to their sex, such as masculinity and stresses pertinent to being a boy or man in our competitive society.
>
> (Van Wormer 2010:17)

In the use of the clause 'of course' Van Wormer seems to anticipate no challenge to this inclusion of gender-sensitive programmes for men, yet her position demands that it be further explored and explained. She writes in favour of gender-sensitive treatment programmes for men and boys which would 'help them work on issues related to their sex, such as masculinity' (Van Wormer 2010:17). Whilst it has certainly been acknowledged within masculinity studies that men are at one and the same time empowered and constrained by their ascribed gender roles, she leaves unsaid what 'issues related to their sex' need to be worked on. She seems too to conflate sex and gender, on the one hand writing of the 'stresses pertinent to being a boy or man' but at the same time referring to the issues raised by masculinity which is a gender-based problem. While Van Wormer's observations in this respect can appear as common-sense extensions of her position on gender-specific programmes more generally, as writers such as Dragiewicz (2011) have articulated this conflation of sex and gender rarely clarifies and instead muddies the conceptual water.

Programmes developed within the rehabilitative arm of the criminal justice system have often homed in on addressing issues surrounding the committing of specific crimes, such as joyriding or graffiti. These programmes have typically sought to divert possible perpetrators away from the commission of crime through engaging perpetrators in a positive relationship with the problem activity, for example teaching car mechanics to joyriders or providing art classes for those who are engaged in graffiti and organising legitimate outlets to replace the illicit. Whilst these programmes have not styled themselves as gender-specific it is clear that they have been largely directed at the behaviours of boys and men, who have proved to be the main instigators of such crimes. Where particular sex- and gender-specific services for men have been more recently formulated these, following the lead of agencies working in development, have tended to concentrate on addressing issues related to masculinity. Within development work, which is by its nature cognisant of varying geographical and political conditions in the country of its application, such programmes have been sensitive to the social, regional and historical contexts and the cultural beliefs and social norms which prevail at any one time and place and which shape local constructions of masculinity (Jobson 2010). Using this knowledge these programmes look to understand the particular ways in which masculinity is achieved and to separate what are considered its positive from its negative effects. In one such example Jobson recounts how an HIV intervention programme for men based in South Africa created 'a livelihood intervention with men [and] a "safe space" in which they could examine their beliefs and behaviours and develop more positive roles for themselves in their families' (Jobson 2010:234). A positive outcome towards gender equality was measured by heightened levels of communication with female partners and a more equal sharing of decision-making in all aspects of household management. These projects, then, involve men in reflecting on their roles within the family, reconsidering dominant constructions of masculinity, reimagining the dynamic between male and female so that power and authority can be shared and establishing an acceptance of the feminine which also encompasses rationality and competency.

Criminology and criminal justice initiatives, however, have traditionally viewed the problem of masculinity as a problem of strain and therefore as a problem related to economy and class. They have considered the problem as that of the inability of men and boys to lead a life in which they can achieve the status of masculinity through positive means such as paid employment or civic participation so that they overcompensate in other areas such as risk-taking, aggression and the subordination of the female (Hall and Winlow 2003). These writers argue that decades of deindustrialisation have led to the disappearance of many avenues to obtain the ideals of hegemonic masculinity to which they aspire, notably to well-paid work for males, and further that neoliberalism has degraded the ethos and experience of community so that men no longer feel that they have a valued place in their neighbourhood. The focus of this theorisation of the problem of masculinity, therefore, has been on reversing the structural violence done to men by an economic and political system which has seen fit to throw men and the industries in which they traditionally gained their independence and self-esteem on a large and growing scrapheap. Feminist scholarship on the other hand has insisted that the problem of masculinity involves the abuse of power by individual males together with forms of structural violence which have an ongoing negative impact on women and girls. Those who call for gender-specific treatment programmes directed at men and boys therefore need to seek clarity as to where the problem of masculinity lies, what its effects are and as to the aims and objectives of such programmes. There is little evidence that these objectives have been fully debated and discussed. Instead the call for gender-specific services for men appears to be based on a preference for the establishment of therapeutic interventions for men and boys. Such interventions can certainly achieve results for individuals but again do little to address the structures of domination and power over the female sex which men and boys can access and can turn to in times of stress. Thus masculinity remains a problem that must continue to be addressed using the feminist lens; without this, the solutions proffered can work to reinforce existing stereotypes and to perpetuate harmful practices towards women and girls.

Note

1 The National March for Abortion Rights was called for and supported by the UK's Trades Union Congress (TUC). It was attended by tens of thousands of male and female trade unionists and their supporters and marked something of a turning point for trade unions nationally. It is usual now for trade unions to have separate women's committees, there is an annual TUC women's conference and equality issues feature within the policy agenda of all TUC-affiliated trade unions in the UK.

References

Cain, M. (1990) 'Towards transgression: new directions in feminist criminology', *International Journal of the Sociology of Law*, 18(1): 1–18.

Channel 4 (2016) 'Episode 1. Hard Men', *All Man*, Channel 4, May.

Connell, R.W. (1987) *Gender and Power: Society, the Person and Sexual Politics.* Stanford, CA: Stanford University Press.

Connell, R.W. (2005) 'Change among the gatekeepers: men, masculinities, and gender equality in the global arena', *Signs*, 30(3): 1801–1825.

Connell, R.W. (2014) 'Margin becoming centre: for a world-centred rethinking of masculinities', *NORMA: International Journal for Masculinity Studies*, 9(4): 217–231.

Connell, R.W. and Messerschmidt, J.W. (2005) 'Hegemonic masculinity: rethinking the concept', *Gender and Society*, 19(6): 829–859.

Carrigan, T., Connell, B. and Lee, J. (1985) 'Toward a new sociology of masculinity', *Theory and Society*, 14(5): 551–604.

Cunningham-Parmeter, K. (2014) '(Un)equal protection: why gender equality depends on discrimination', *Northwestern University Law Review*, 109(1): 1–56.

Dragiewicz, M. (2011) *Equality with a Vengeance: Men's Rights Groups, Battered Women, and Antifeminist Backlash.* Boston, MA: Northeastern University Press.

Dragiewicz, M. and Mann, R.M. (2016) 'Fighting feminism – organised opposition to women's rights: guest editors' introduction', *International Journal for Crime, Justice and Social Democracy*, 5(2): 1–5.

Faludi, S. (1991) *Backlash: The Undeclared War against Women.* London: Vintage Books.

Flood, M. (2005) 'Father's rights', in Flood, M., Gardiner, J.K., Pease, B. and Pringle, K. (eds), *The International Encyclopedia of Men and Masculinities.* London: Routledge.

Hall, S. and Winlow, S. (2003) 'Culture, gender and male violence: a key problem', *Criminal Justice Matters*, 53(1): 14–15.

Hartmann, H. (1979) 'The unhappy marriage of Marxism and feminism: towards a more progressive union?', *Capital and Class*, 8: 1–33.

Holter, O.G. (2005) 'Social theories for researching men and masculinities: direct gender hierarchy and structural inequality', in Kimmel, M.S., Hearn, J. and Connell, R.W. (eds), *Handbook of Studies on Men and Masculinities.* London: Sage, pp. 15–34.

Jobson, G. (2010) 'Changing masculinities: land-use, family communication and prospects for working with older men towards gender equality in a livelihoods intervention', *Culture, Health & Sexuality*, 12(3): 233–246.

Kimmel, M.S. and Messner, M.A. (eds) (2010) *Men's Lives.* Boston, MA: Allyn and Bacon.

Kivel, P. (1999) *Boys Will Be Men: Raising Our Sons for Courage, Caring, and Community.* Gabriola Island, BC: New Society Publishers.

Kruttschnitt, C. (1982) 'Respectable women and the law', *The Sociological Quarterly*, 23(2): 221–234.

McCarry, M. (2007) 'Masculinity studies and male violence: critique or collusion?', *Women's Studies International Forum*, 30(5): 404–415.

Mann, M., Menih, H. and Smith, C. (2014) 'There is "hope for you yet": the female drug offender in sentencing discourse', *Australian and New Zealand Journal of Criminology*, 47(3): 355–373.

Marinova, J. (2003) 'Gender stereotypes and the socialization process', United Nations Division for the Advancement of Women (DAW), www.un.org/womenwatch/daw/egm/men-boys2003/EP3-Marinova.pdf [Accessed 27 July 2016].

Mattsson, T. (2015) '"Good girls": emphasised femininity as cloning culture in academia', *Gender and Education*, 27(6): 685–699.

Morrell, R. and Swart, S. (2005) 'Men in the third world: postcolonial perspectives on masculinity', in Kimmel, M.S., Hearn, J. and Connell, R.W. (eds), *Handbook of Studies on Men and Masculinities.* London: Sage, pp. 90–113.

Robinson, V. (2003) 'Radical revisionings? The theorizing of masculinity and (radical) feminist theory', *Women's Studies International Forum*, 26(2): 129–137.

Rowbotham, S., Segal, L. and Wainwright, H. (1979) *Beyond the Fragments: Feminism and the Making of Socialism.* London: Merlin Press.

Sargent, L. and Hartmann, H.I. (1986) *The Unhappy Marriage of Marxism and Feminism: A Debate of Class and Patriarchy.* London: Pluto Press.

Segal, L. (1989) 'Slow change or no change? Feminism, socialism and the problem of men', *Feminist Review*, 31(1): 5–21.

Skeggs, B. (1997) *Formations of Class & Gender: Becoming Respectable.* London: Sage.

Stanko, E.A. (1992) 'The case of fearful women: gender, personal safety and fear of crime', *Women and Criminal Justice*, 4(1): 117–135.

UN (2001) 'Supporting gender mainstreaming', Office of the Special Adviser on Gender Issues and Advancement of Women, United Nations, www.un.org/womenwatch/osagi/pdf/report.pdf [Accessed 28 July 2016].

UN (2014) 'UN rights panels outline states' obligation to prevent harmful practices on women, girls', *UN News Centre*, 5 November, www.un.org/apps/news/story.asp?NewsID=49254 [Accessed 27 July 2016].

Van Wormer, K. (2010) *Working with Female Offenders: A Gender-Sensitive Approach.* Hoboken, NJ: John Wiley and Sons.

Walby, S. (1988) *Gender Segregation at Work.* Milton Keynes: Open University Press.

Walby, S. (1990) *Theorizing Patriarchy.* Oxford: Basil Blackwell.

Chapter 5

Gender-responsive justice

Critical appraisals

The discussion in Chapter 4 revealed that gender-responsive justice has come under sustained criticism from conservative forces in society such as the men's rights movement. This chapter looks at criticisms of gender-responsive justice which flow from more radical and critical perspectives. There are a number of significant facets to these criticisms which will be explored in this chapter. First to be discussed will be critiques which have been inspired and constructed from a feminist perspective – many of these critiques are largely sympathetic to the ideals of gender-responsive justice, but feel that it has been poorly executed. Then the latter part of the chapter will look at critiques which have been more hostile to the idea of gender-responsive justice, either because its critics believe that the focus on gender is either problematic or partial or because they take an abolitionist position which contends that systems of criminal justice cannot be successfully reformed and must be entirely abandoned and replaced with more radical, revolutionary alternatives which respond to issues raised by those who break the law.

Feminism and the critique of gender-responsive justice

By the early years of the twenty-first century the practice of gender-responsive justice had become established in a number of regions across the globe. The growing population of female prisoners and the increase in women and girls coming into contact with the criminal justice system had inspired a growth in the availability of programmes which set out to work differently with females who had broken the law. Alongside the growth of provision for females an increase in research and evaluations of the programmes offered to women and girls began to appear in the literature. At this point the language of gender-responsive justice, rather than women-centred or gender-specific programming, had been firmly established, reflecting the wider restructuring of 'offender-management' along the principles of risk, need and responsivity which had transformed work with law-breakers across much of the Western world (Hannah-Moffat 2008). The growth in gender-responsive interventions required that they be evaluated and compared to more mainstream programmes in order to assess their efficiency and their effectiveness. Many of the studies were generally supportive of the gender-responsive requirement to include a different set of provisions which took into account the specific needs of females and argued that there was a continuing need for the development of specialised programmes and interventions for the female population (Hall et al. 2011). However, at the same time gender-responsive interventions were held up to a more critical evaluation which raised questions concerning both the theory and practice of programmes which focused on women's differences.

1 Does gender-responsive justice reinforce existing social relations of gender?

An early and significant critique of gender-responsive justice maintained that in its practice gender-responsive justice might be unwittingly reinforcing the very inequalities which the proponents of a gender-centred lens had highlighted as problematic. Evidence began to emerge to suggest that many gender-responsive programmes were guilty of working with women in a way which reinforced gendered stereotypes limiting the role of women in society. A multinational study reporting in 1999 found that:

> programs intentionally designed to embody the ideals of gender-responsive programming in fact did the opposite. Limiting and damaging gender stereotypes were reinforced in the name of gender-responsive programming.
>
> (Morash 2010:11)

These programmes were based on acknowledging, but not necessarily challenging existing differences, so worked with the extant stereotypes rather than against them. Morash has highlighted that in the absence of alternatives gender-responsive programmes can fall back on misleading stereotypes about the roles and motivations of women service users. They have, for example, been found guilty of seeing women as parents first with the individual woman's needs afforded a secondary importance to that of their child; of providing therapeutic sessions for women which seek to meet the emotional and spiritual needs of women to the neglect of more focused, expert interventions such as psychological interventions and vocational training; and of neglecting more practical needs such as women's greater need as substance users (Erez 1989, Buffard and Taxman 2000, Mullany 2002 in Morash 2010). Morash has also observed a number of programmes for women which, much like Bentham's Sotinium, include blatantly stereotypical training opportunities in skills which are considered appropriately feminine such as in flower arranging, cookery or sewing, skills which would never or rarely feature in programmes delivered to men.

The fact that such programmes exist for women in the gender-responsive sector of course does not prove that the entire philosophy behind it is inherently flawed. If Morash and others found such programmes made up the entirety of what gender-responsive interventions had to offer then such a criticism would be entirely apt, however this is not the case. As Morash also shows, the success of many gender-responsive programmes is that they often offer what is termed a *wraparound* or *holistic* service which engages multiple providers to address the many needs of the women under their supervision. They will also often provide a *continuum of care* which ensures that the programmes offered for women are continually reviewed and updated as their needs change at different stages of their rehabilitation. There are many examples of good practice which have been provided within gender-responsive treatment programmes and which follow the principles set out by Bloom, Covington and others in the early years, but provision still remains patchy. Programming which is delivered under the rubric of gender-responsivity, as much research reveals, is likely not to deliver to the standards and principles of its ideal type and may not deliver the conceptual shift in its approach to women who break the law which would be required to deliver more positive, liberating and empowering outcomes for the women under its care.

Perhaps a more interesting and foundationally challenging aspect of this critique is that raised by Hannah-Moffat (2010), amongst others, who have argued that a foundational emphasis on gender difference creates its own conceptual and practical difficulties. The gender-responsive approach, Hannah-Moffat argues, is based on the acceptance that there is a fundamental difference between the experiences and psychological development of women and of men. It is this foundational principle which can easily lead to stereotypical assumptions being made about the nature of offenders and consequently as to their subsequent needs. This acceptance of difference leads itself to stereotypical characterisations and to 'implicit normative assumptions routinely made about women' (and also no doubt about men) (Hannah-Moffat 2010:198). The focus on females in the development of gender-responsive theorisation has meant that it is women whose choices and motivations have been interrogated and explored as different. This approach means that once again it is women's needs which are conceived of as out of step and it is women as a sex who are considered as requiring special treatment.

As the needs of women are further explored and a sensitivity to women as gendered beings becomes a more usual approach to take, this can culminate in the development of an alternative set of norms to which women are expected to aspire and to achieve. These expectations can be dangerous to women in a number of ways, first by setting women up for failure if they do not conform to the alternative norms set out for them, and secondly these alternates can become set in stone so that the fluid and changeable nature of gender subjectivities is lost and women are expected to conform to patterns of gender behaviour which have become 'accepted' and subsequently ossified. As

Hannah-Moffat (2010) clearly articulates, correctional systems which have adapted to these different expectations are likely to consider diversion from these newly constituted norms as problematic behaviour and this can subsequently lead to the harsher treatment of females in the courts rather than resulting in a sensitivity to the individual and her changing needs. Women and girls may consequently be subjected to requirements set by a gender-responsive system which also limit their behaviour but in ways which are far more subtle and difficult to detect than the more obviously stereotypical expectations which previously prevailed.

2 Gender-responsive programmes as an administrative solution to structural problems?

Hannah-Moffat (2010) makes a powerful argument that gender-responsive principles have been well-intentioned but that their poor theorisation has had unintended consequences so that as a result the title of gender-responsive has 'been attached to a wide range of improvised and poorly adapted programs and managerial processes' (196). Advocates of gender-responsive programming, she argues, have based their approach on empirical gender differences revealed through two central theories which maintain that there is a fundamental difference between the ways that the lives of men and women are led. Relational theory contends that women gain their sense of identity and self-esteem through their relationships with others, while men are more self-contained and gain their own feelings of self-worth in more individualised ways. Secondly, pathways theory maintains that women's motivations and pathways to offending differ from men's because women face a different set of adversities related to their vulnerability as women, inhabiting women's bodies and being positioned in a social framework which is dominated by patriarchal values and the demeaning of women's experiences. These vulnerabilities, it is argued, cannot therefore be experienced by men who are very differently positioned. A further set of theories – trauma and addictions theories – then contend that services provided to women must be developed to take into account these different experiences. They must be trauma-informed, recognising the deep harms which many women have suffered as a consequence of the ongoing discrimination and oppressive practices which they routinely face, and they must offer a therapeutic approach which offers a supportive and caring response to the problems which women present.

While the adoption of these theoretical approaches can offer certain advantages to women, replacing judgemental, punitive and controlling responses with those which seek to understand the context in which women come to the attention of the criminal justice system and to tailor responses accordingly, in practice they are often poorly understood. The empirical differences which these theories have revealed are described but not adequately explained, Hannah-Moffat (2010) argues, leaving significant gaps in the knowledge and understanding of the problems faced by women. As they stand at present then, theories which inform gender-responsive practice help us to understand 'what works' with women who break the law and how individual women respond to the harms of the criminal justice system in practice. They can also help practitioners and policy-makers understand that women respond in different ways to men and that programmes should take the different experiences of women into account if they want to be successful in supporting women to make different choices in the future. These are admirable goals, but they are limited to outcomes which improve the efficiency of existing administrative procedures and systems. These are theories which seek to better understand the empirical realities in which women's lives are led and to intervene better with that knowledge, but they do not seek to change those realities or to ultimately alter the conditions which women endure in society more generally, which underpin and severely limit their decision-making and which also create the conditions in which women find themselves in conflict with the law. As a consequence they can make a difference to women individually, providing them with better coping mechanisms or improved emotional resilience, or helping to solve some of the immediate practical problems which led to their law-breaking such as homelessness, violence or lack of economic resources, but they cannot impact in the longer term on changing the social conditions which so often drag women down and increase their vulnerability to social harms. As with all administrative solutions they can improve the effectiveness of reactive interventions but cannot intervene successfully in the social world in order to change the conditions in which women suffer structural and personal violence. They are, in short, solutions offered from the perspective of liberal feminist praxis which offers improved access to services and the development of programmes which are sensitive to gender and inequality but which ultimately do not seek to overturn the conditions which are at the root cause of that inequality. Moreover it is also an approach which allows only for individual adjustment to extant conditions – which can be undertaken by those who are given the opportunity to participate in a relevant programme – but which offers no possibility of collective resistance which could change conditions for the many. As such, gender-responsive programmes will continue to face criticism from feminists of a more radical persuasion.

3 Can gender-responsive theory really make a difference to criminal justice practice?

As we have seen, gender-responsive perspectives aim to improve the outcomes for women who have entered systems of criminal justice and to reduce the harms which women suffer within systems of care, control and punishment. These systems, the perspective holds, have previously been framed in masculinist terms and are not fit for purpose when applied to the female sex. However, there is mounting evidence to suggest that gender-responsive programmes, while they may be welcomed by individual women for many reasons, may be making less of a difference to systems of justice than they claim. First there is the matter of numbers. The rise in interest in and application of gender-responsive programmes has coincided with an unprecedented increase in the number of women and girls sentenced and there is no evidence to suggest that programmes which are sensitive to gender and to the needs of women have had any impact in reducing the numbers coming into contact with the criminal justice system. Secondly there is the matter of impact on the quality of services available to women. While there has been an explosion of literature on the subject of gender-responsive interventions and of opportunities for training in its principles, in the attention paid to the treatment of women who break the law and in the creation of relevant policy in this area, there remain numerous problems in the ways that gender-responsive principles have been interpreted by many organisations charged with the delivery of gender-sensitive programming for women. Finally there is the charge that gender-responsive programming has been unable to transform the masculinist principles which continue to form the basic ordering of systems of criminal justice and of punishment regimes.

i The question of numbers

The numbers of women and girls who come into contact with the criminal justice system at any time in their lives began to grow steadily from the 1980s. There are many reasons for this growth which it is not the purpose of this chapter to outline but it is important to acknowledge that this growth cannot be easily explained and is as much a product of the raised profile of women and girls in society more generally as of any evidence that they are more prone to criminality. Much of this increase in the criminalisation of women and girls was recorded in the US, where in April 2014 as many as 1.2 million women and girls were under the supervision of the criminal justice system – either incarcerated or subject to penalties in the community. Between 1980 and 2014 the rate of growth of female imprisonment in the US outpaced that for men by more than 50 per cent and it was the goal of the advocates for gender-responsive justice that this unprecedented rise should be interrogated, critiqued and reversed. While there is some evidence that the rate of growth of women's imprisonment has slowed somewhat in the US over the last decade (particularly the rate of incarceration of African American females), the overall numbers of women overall who have been brought into the criminal justice net, and who are subject to imprisonment as a result, continue to rise (The Sentencing Project 2015).

From a global perspective the UN has raised specific concerns over what it describes as 'a significant rise in the rate of women's imprisonment in many countries worldwide' (United Nations Office on Drugs and Crime 2014:2). Much of this increase they attribute to a trend for authorities to deliver a tougher stance against crime, a trend which can be seen worldwide with more legislation enacted which criminalises more activities, the turn to crime control rather than the provision of welfare to those in need and the increasing severity of punishment regimes, particularly for those who have committed drug-related offences. In addition the UN has detected an increase in religious codes and laws being used against women committing offences: what are termed 'moral crimes'. These may include such actions as the breaking of strict dress-codes, being seen in a public place without an appropriate chaperone or running away from a troubled home (United Nations Office on Drugs and Crime 2014:4). Turning this around, they suggest, will need successful action in many areas including mainstreaming gender equality in all policies, laws, procedures, programmes and practices which ensure that women and girls have access to justice; diverting women from prosecution whenever possible; gender-sensitive training of law enforcement officials; ending pre-trial detention for women unless not to do so would place others at risk but always where this is practised as a form of protective custody; taking caring responsibilities into consideration when assessing the appropriateness of detention; the decriminalisation of many drug offences and the removal of mandatory sentencing for all drug offences; and bringing all legislation in line with international standards which guard against gender discrimination. It is clear from this long, yet still incomplete, list of recommendations that achieving the goal of reducing the criminalisation and the imprisonment of women and girls requires a seismic shift in social attitudes and changes in legislation, the practices of the state and in policy implementation. Unfortunately progress in one area can easily be outweighed by intransigence and reversals in others.

As it stands, the trend towards increasingly punitive sanctions and the widening of the criminal justice net seem to be having a greater impact on numbers sentenced and imprisoned than ever before. The advocates of gender-responsive treatment must acknowledge the magnitude of the problem before them and seek solutions which will impact at the most significant levels if they are to reverse these trends which are so detrimental to the female sex. This will require a critique of law and order rhetorics and policy, the decentring of crime within governance strategies and a reframing and reimagining of the ideas of criminalisation and punishment which drive so much social and individual harm (Gelsthorpe 2013).

ii The problem of therapeutic punishment

As we have seen in earlier chapters, the social control of women and girls means that they are subject to excessive forms of regulation both in their daily lives and through the various workings of the institutions of the state. Those females who step outside of these limited boundaries are subjected to greater forms of control and punishment than are men. This is true within both formal and informal regulatory frameworks. There is plenty of evidence to demonstrate that girls are more likely than boys to be held to particular moral and behavioural standards. Ideals of femininity constrain and limit behaviour, whilst those attached to masculinity open up the world to boys and men, suggesting that few boundaries to their behaviour exist. Girls and young women are especially vulnerable to close monitoring and even to institutionalisation as a result of statutory intervention which is pre-crime in its approach. The female sex is more likely to come to the attention of the authorities as a consequence of what are known as 'status offences' – actions which are not necessarily criminal in their own right but which nevertheless raise concerns when they are carried out by certain groups and are prohibited or censured as a result. Girls are much more likely to be removed from their families and confined in correctional institutions for running away from home, defying authority or for fighting, for example, than are boys. In short the 'survival strategies' of young women and girls continue to be criminalised (Gordoliza 2013). There is evidence too that adult women are also more likely to face harsher penalties than men and for similar reasons. Women may be sentenced to correctional treatment either in the community or even in prison 'for their own good' but where men would be differently dealt with by the courts (Gregory 1986). The decision to refer women to correctional agencies in these particular circumstances can betray an overly paternalistic attitude towards women, where the sentencer is motivated by (usually his) concern for the woman's welfare. This over-sentencing can also result from a belief that the 'experts' know better than the woman herself what is in her best interests. Such decisions can reflect more widely held beliefs that strip women of their power and agency outside of the penal system. The 'up-tariffing' of women in the criminal justice system has been noted in a number of studies (Easton et al. 2010, Hedderman 2010). Paradoxically the availability of gender-responsive treatment options can contribute to this tendency to up-tariff. As Mills and others have observed:

> If sentencers believe that prison is a place where women will get appropriate help, they may engage in 'therapeutic sentencing', or, as Pat Carlen (2002) might say 'therapunitive sentencing' – sending women to prison to receive such help.
>
> (Mills, Barocas and Ariel 2013:59)

The inclination to use the criminal justice system and its sentencing provision to place women in 'protective custody' is likely to be exacerbated where cutbacks have removed sources of support which could previously be accessed outside the criminal justice system as welfare or health-related needs. The creeping criminalisation of social policy which has been detected as a growing feature of governmentality across many neoliberal societies has especially exacerbated this particular problem in the last decade or so. Resources are routinely diverted away from those in need of welfare support and funnelled instead to those considered as a criminal risk, even diverting funds from community-based to in-prison services, in the name of efficiency and effective interventions (Mills, Barocas and Ariel 2013:59). As Sheehan (2013:13) reports, there is a real danger that prison might be considered 'as the new social services' and that women will continue to be incarcerated in greater numbers as a consequence.

iii The dominance of (women-centred) control

It is clear that there is a pressing need for an improvement in the treatment of women and girls throughout systems of criminal justice; too often these systems humiliate, label and harm women who come through their doors. Any moves to treat women and girls with more sensitivity and empathy need to be encouraged and hailed as significant victories. However, while there are many examples which demonstrate that a gender-responsive approach can result in much better outcomes for women and girls there is also evidence to suggest that treatment offered under this label can be littered with examples of poor practice. Sometimes these interventions are justified as opening up significant and necessary opportunities for women when in practice they merely present new ways of controlling women and their behaviour. Unfortunately it is not difficult to find examples of interventions which have been labelled as gender-responsive but which raise troubling questions.

Hannah-Moffat (2010) uses the examples of problematic policies devised inside prisons which have been ostensibly developed to give women improved access to their children. While initially conceived as essential to ensuring that the pains of imprisonment and separation are reduced for mother and child, that family connections are maintained and that the rights of the mother are respected whatever her residential circumstances, access to children became a tool to more effectively regulate women's behaviour. The threat of withdrawal of the mother's rights to be with her child was used as a method of ensuring the mother's conformity to certain prescribed behaviours as well as programme goals and outcomes. This callous misuse of deeply held maternal feelings and emotions served as an example of an institutionalised form of coercive control. It closely mirrored the abuses which many women in prison report that they have had to endure on the outside and which gender-sensitive and women-centred approaches were designed to eliminate. Instead, in this example, sensitivity to a woman's bond with her children was used as a form of psychological control as violent as any other use of physical or mental force wielded to ensure adherence to institutional rules and instructions.

Such measures of control can become so normalised and routinely applied within institutions that they can appear unproblematic, and even as caring or empowering, to those who devise and instigate them. In May 2012 a panel on gender-responsive practice delivered to the Second Chances and Safer Communities conference held in Washington, DC, offered a useful example as to how the care of women can in practice turn to their surveillance and over-regulation. The women, all policy-makers and practitioners, who presented on their work in this area declared a commitment to implementing gender-responsive approaches in their work in prisons and community corrections in the US, and while claiming their effectiveness and sensitivity to women's needs, yet certain of their practices could also appear to include elements which are troubling and also possibly anti-women. The presentations focused on the responsibility of individual women, as well as systems of correction, to be held to account for their actions and to take responsibility for their behaviour yet the practice on the ground which they outlined appeared clearly focused on the individual woman and her abilities alone and without further reflection as to how the function of corrections and imprisonment might militate against women's empowerment and agency. One presenter gave an example of the importance of the prison-based nursery programmes and mother and baby units at the prison in which she worked. While reinforcing the importance of the creation of a non-prison-like environment within which the mother and child could bond, she happily and unreflexively explained that cameras monitored the baby's cot on a 24-hour basis in order to ensure the safety of the infant. This measure was presented as an enabling device rather than being perceived as a breach of the mother's right to privacy and as a further extension of control over the mother's behaviour which in effect mirrors the damage meted out to women subject to excessive surveillance and coercion in society more generally. There was no consideration in the presentation as to how this constant surveillance might affect the mother's own sense of safety and security. It is clear that the institutional needs of the prison had been placed before those of the woman and that a policy which set out to be woman-centred in its design had become prison-centred in its delivery (The National Re-entry Resource Centre 2012). As Kendall and Pollack (2005) have found in their own research on women-centred mental health programming in prison:

> the tension between offering support services to women in prison and the possibility that these services will be complicit in perpetuating the regulation of women prisoners is a challenging one.
>
> (83)

Kendall and Pollack's research has raised a number of issues concerning the reforms carried out in Canada subsequent to their 'women-centred' turn in policy in the 1990s. The Correctional Service of Canada, they write, has received international attention and praise for its reforms which closed Canada's only federal prison for women and replaced it with five more locally based prison facilities which were to be based on feminist healing principles and the empowerment of women in prison. In practice, however, inside the new facilities services designed to improve the mental health of female prisoners follow a psychological discourse which serves to regulate and 'tame' rather than to empower or support (Kendall and Pollack 2005:72).

iv The persistence of punishment

Gender-responsive options are, at the end of the day, often financed and directed by organisations which are firmly located in correctional programming and can begin to follow the principles of correction rather than those which might result in improved justice for women. Concern to develop provision which is centred on the needs of women can easily metamorphose into provision to contain offenders who happen to be female and which is built on existing male-centred and masculinist blueprints. Lawston and Meiners (2014) revealed, for example, that a network of facilities for female prisoners in California which was initially envisioned under the auspices of gender-responsive programming in effect became another element in plans for the expansion of the prison system in that state. Initial promises that the facilities would be constructed as local centres which would be community-run were replaced with plans to utilise the state's existing Department of Corrections and Facilities instead. This significant shift, which was money-saving in its intention, in reality signalled that a very different outcome, and one which would have expanded the prison estate, was preferred instead.

As Lawston and Meiners argue, even in the best outcomes, women who have come into conflict with the law are not released from the clutches of the state as a consequence of the provision of gender-responsive programmes. While the best plans might result in the site of their control and correction being altered from the penal estate to the community and while the methods utilised may differ from traditional practices of control and coercion, in many gender-responsive programmes women are still subjected to punitive sanctions and held individually responsible for their response to a set of circumstances which are located in structural inequalities which clearly lie outside their control. In a similar vein to their treatment in more traditional settings, women continue to be further sanctioned if they are seen to be unresponsive to the correctional environment and unwilling (rather than unable) to conform to the expectations of whichever punitive regime they are located within. Indeed the contradictions and tensions between the discourse of woman-centred and gender-responsive programmes and the realities of prison and correctional environments have been 'thoroughly critiqued' in recent years (Kendall and Pollack 2005:73–74).

v Women and the risk agenda

The last two decades has seen the predominance of risk-based management of offenders in many correctional settings across the globe. This shift to actuarial principles in managing those who break the law can be seen as a rejection of the liberal ideals which suggest that individuals can be rehabilitated given the correct support and advice (Silvestri and Crowther-Dowey 2016:88). These offender-management perspectives are in many ways anathema to the principles of gender-responsive justice where women are treated as people in need of individualised care and support to help them to unravel the particular circumstances which have led them into the commission of crime. Instead risk assessment sees individuals assessed, aggregated into low- or high-risk categories and subjected to a raft of existing programmes to manage their behaviour depending on their perceived dangers to society. Attention to the whole person and their complex circumstances and needs is sacrificed to the parameters of the risk assessment tools which have been devised to aid the categorisation of service-users into groups. The shift to risk-based interventions has also been seen as a rejection of the proportionality principle in that individuals are slotted into programmes not so much based on the acts they have committed in the past as on the risk they might pose in the future. These are crude tools indeed, especially when applied to the complexities of women's lives where victimisation and the commission of crime are inseparably intertwined.

In the hands of the risk assessment tools women's complex needs are translated into ongoing and significant risks and women are accordingly required to successfully complete programmes which have been devised for the high-risk offender and to demonstrate that they are willing and able to turn their lives around as a consequence. Hudson (2002) has argued that these new frameworks led to an increased use of short-term prison sentences for women in England and Wales as magistrates did not focus on the nature of the crimes women were convicted for (which were low-level, non-violent offences), but instead fixed their attention onto the intransigence of many of the problems faced by women. Unable to intervene to change the circumstances in which women were making their decisions, magistrates, in their zeal to *do something*, turned to sentencing options instead in order to try to make women see sense and make the necessary changes in their lives. Poteat (2002:126) similarly concluded that this turn to individual accountability and responsibilisation has led to women becoming 'the fastest growing population nationally in prisons and locally in jails' as they prove unable to overcome the many obstacles present in their lives or to conform to the behaviours expected of them in society more generally. In essence women in both the UK and the US are being held responsible for not addressing the circumstances of their own victimisation, poverty or oppression – a classic case once again of blaming the victim.

In the light of the evidence demonstrating the extremely patchy and problematic experience of women-centred risk assessments in the US, advocates of gender-responsive justice should have rejected the use of risk-needs assessments wholesale as anathema to their foundational principles. Even in terms of practical applications these tools have been shown to be inadequate in assessing women's needs and in delivering support which is tailored to the circumstances of women as individuals or indeed as an entire social group. A number of feminist writers have revealed the masculinist assumptions on which the assessments of risk are based and have argued for the abandonment of such practices where women are concerned (Hudson 2002, Hannah-Moffat 2002, 2010). However, in a correctional environment which has been dominated by risk assessment tools and practices there has been a move to adapt these tools to gender-sensitive and 'women-friendly' perspectives. The advocates of gender-responsive correctional programming, cognisant of the critiques of risk-based approaches for women and girls, have sought to devise new tests which can be more sensitively applied to women and girls and which include 'information about histories of domestic violence, sexual abuse, mental illness, self-esteem, and parental responsibilities' within the instruments of assessment (Hannah-Moffat 2010:201). This exercise has presented multiple problems. Both the ethics and efficacy of adapting such a masculinist approach for use on women have been questioned (Mills, Barocas and Ariel 2013) and there has been criticism of the design and application of assessment tools which claim to be gender-responsive but which have proved as blunt an instrument as those devised based on androcentric experiences and principles.

Gender-responsive risk assessments have been described as 'commercialised feminism' (Hannah-Moffat 2010:201) and a lucrative industry has been created around their use and offering training in their application. In addition their delivery can attract essential resources to those community and voluntary organisations which are called upon to deliver such programmes on behalf of the state. They remain, however, firmly wedded to a particular view of change which stresses individual routes out of oppression and in addition have been criticised for their inadequate understanding of the needs and experiences of women living on the margins of society and affected by poverty and racism, instead 'drawing on knowledge and experiences of white middle-class women to produce normative criteria against which criminalised women and girls are judged' (Hannah-Moffat 2010:201). As Hannah-Moffat also outlines, these are instruments which are decontextualised, lacking sufficient attention to the oppressive practices which women and girls face on a daily basis, interpreting any aggression or violence exhibited as offensive and unacceptable when it could be interpreted as defensive and reasonable in the light of the context of the woman's life overall. Defiance towards authority can be similarly categorised as problematic behaviour rather than as demonstrating individual agency and power, dissent or resistance to institutional violence and harm.

Hannah-Moffat outlines many further problems associated with gender-responsive risk assessment tools. She acknowledges that:

> Female-specific classification may be 'better' than male-based risk instruments at dividing and classifying female populations for the purposes of correctional management. However, this classification method is still

> fundamentally restricted by its strict adherence to a statistically-based risk framework that cannot provide a holistic perspective of women's diversity, criminalisation, institutional behaviour or treatment needs. Technical correctional definitions of need are legitimated and authorised by science, not by individuals' lay assessment of their circumstances.
>
> (Hannah-Moffat 2010:204)

In addition she notes that the number of women in the US who were categorised by these programmes as 'high-risk' doubled between 1997 and 2006 and that this increase occurred since the development of gender-responsive risk assessments.

4 Is gender-responsive policy under-theorised?

Policy frameworks do not lend themselves particularly well to the subtleties and complexities required by feminist approaches. The carefully argued and crafted positions which have been constructed through decades of feminist theorising can become lost in translation as they are adapted to fit the requirements of policy-makers and practitioners. While the latter may also be guided by feminist perspectives and principles and motivated by the desire to transfer these to the frontline of service-delivery, they operate in a cruder arena dominated by sound-bite politics and the need to explain and 'sell' a shift in practice to a wider audience. In these circumstances the principles of gender-sensitivity and women-centred provision can become trapped in limiting statements concerning what women want or need. These statements are in danger of forever fixing the identity of the female sex as 'relational, victimised, maternal, nurturing and disadvantaged' (Hannah-Moffat 2010:198) and of denying females any alternative subjectivities. As Kegan Gardiner counsels:

> The most important accomplishment of 20th century feminist theory is … the idea that masculinity and femininity are loosely defined, historically variable, and interrelated social ascriptions to persons with certain kinds of bodies – not the natural, necessary, or ideal characteristics of people with similar genitals.
>
> (Kegan Gardiner 2005:35)

Once adopted into policy and practice the, admittedly more sensitive, understandings of the female condition which have been revealed by women-centred research and reflection can become inscribed as into stone, forever wedded to experiences which may in reality have been time-limited and changeable in practice, and the variability and changeability of women's experiences can easily be lost. While initially adopted for the best of reasons and to guard against gender discrimination, principled approaches can transform into rigid policy objectives which take on an immovable character and which are unable to adapt to the particular circumstances faced by individual women or to the changing situations in which women and girls find that they have space to operate. In addition, the differences between male and female can more easily become essentialised in their translation to the policy context so that statements made about the needs of 'women and girls' can suggest that all individuals ascribed the status of female share the same experiences, understandings and adaptations to a common condition as a consequence of sharing common biological characteristics. As a consequence there have been a number of feminist critiques of gender-responsive practices within which the critics have considered that women are disadvantaged by such an approach as they are shoehorned into a different set of expectations and normative frameworks, stereotyped as needy, weak and vulnerable. While this may act as an improvement on previous characterisations of women who break the law as inherently dangerous and evil, they present their own problems and limitations (Kendall 2002, Hannah-Moffat 2010).

5 What about intersectionality?

The model of gender-responsive treatment places gender discrimination at the core of a woman's experiences. As a consequence this foregrounding of gender can marginalise other crucial aspects of individual experience which can equally shape individual identity and lived reality, such as class, race, sexuality, ability and so on (Lawston and Meiners 2014). The lives of those women and girls who are sentenced are shaped by more than the sex category which they have been ascribed. They are more likely also to be impoverished, working class, women of colour and in poor mental and physical health. All these material realities contribute to the circumstances which bring women and girls to the attention of the courts and whilst these conditions are inextricably interwoven with gender, victimisation and vulnerability they cannot be subsumed under the one overarching category of woman. To do so risks denying the complex, multilayered nature of the oppression faced by women, much of which can be said to be shared but not all. Added to this mix of oppressive practices in recent years is the realisation that the ascription of a biological sex category can itself act as a form of violence and can elicit further oppression to those who identify outside of socially ascribed gender categories, as trans, non-binary or queer. Those who do not place themselves within cisgender categorisations are subjected to further forms of violence and harm by a system which appears inflexible and disinterested in the experiences of fluidity, non-conforming gender identities or any other than a heteronormative sexuality. Existing models of gender-responsive practice, however, 'make[…] essentialist assumptions about who "counts" as women' (Lawston 2013:113) and thereby 'erase[…]' the experiences of women whose gender identity has been changed from that which they were ascribed at birth. Some feminists deny those alternate experiences and argue against the rights of trans females to be considered as women (Stark 2015). Furthermore, as war, poverty and politics fuel the widespread movement and displacement of people around the globe it is also imperative to consider the position of the migrant, their increasing criminalisation and the fact that many detained and incarcerated women and girls will also face the added factor of being locked away in foreign countries with language and cultural barriers to contend with as well as the threat of forced deportation.

As Lawston and Meiners (2014) propose, the greater understanding which the gendered pathways to crime literature has fostered should be supplemented and extended further to take into account the particular circumstances faced by the groups of women who are most often made the objects of attention and punishment throughout the penal system and carceral state more widely. As they call to our attention:

> The gendered pathways to crime approach has done well to expose how high rates of violence and poverty are closely connected to women's crime and incarceration. It has been very useful for contextualizing, for theorists and activists alike, the circumstances that lead to women's imprisonment. But the approach is limited, in that it does not fully account for the ways in which gender, race, and sexuality coalesce so that *certain* women and girls are *targeted* by the criminal justice system for incarceration.
>
> (Lawston and Meiners 2014:6, italics in original)

Lawston and Meiners add another crucial element to the gendered pathways approach and this is to consider the power of the state in the criminalisation of women and girls. The carceral state does not merely reflect and institutionalise existing discriminatory practices but also constructs the frameworks within which certain populations are profiled and marked out as problematic. The state then controls the means through which such groups are regulated and serviced, or denied access to services, and in so doing creates the criminogenic conditions within which women and girls are forced to operate and struggle to survive and prosper. The growth of neoliberalism across the globe has been associated with a rise in poverty and inequality, the withdrawal of welfare provision and the diversion of resources away from those in need, all trends which have hit women, and women of colour particularly, very hard. With the added burden of race discrimination which further blocks opportunities at every turn, survival for many women and girls depends upon engagement in some of the most marginal areas of the economy – in the sex industry, drug trafficking and selling goods in the informal and illicit economy (Alfred and Chlup 2009). These are represented as individualised decisions which are freely taken as the legal and penal system is based on the premise of rationality and personal choice. These systems do not recognise the structural violences and constraints on individual action which severely limit the choices which are available; as a consequence punishments are handed out to those who face the most barriers to surviving. Mauer and Chesney-Lind (2002) have even declared that crime and welfare policy in the US can be perceived as a war on communities of colour, with this war extended outside the criminal justice system and into the workings of social and welfare services.

It is clear from this analysis that it is problematic for feminists to work too closely alongside the state without exposing its part in victimising so many women. Feminist criminology, in its theory and in its practice, falls short of championing the rights of women if it does not incorporate an analysis of the state and its particular discriminatory practices. It should concern itself not only with how the carceral state treats women in their regulation, sentencing and punishment, but also with how the state and the institutions which represent it subject the female sex to forms of structural violence and create and extend discriminatory and oppressive practices across the life-cycle. It is important too that the injustices of racism are taken fully into account, not only in the ways in which racialised individuals and their communities are treated once they enter systems of criminal justice but in understanding the ways in which women of colour, migrants and those categorised as 'foreign' continuously face discriminatory practices which cut off their possibilities for action and which condemn them to desperate circumstances despite their skills, education and motivation to succeed.

Gender-responsive perspectives will not impact on the lives of women if they do not embrace the need for structural change but instead concentrate on individualised strategies and personal points of transformation. Furthermore it is important that gender-responsive justice models develop and adapt to take into consideration the contribution which queer criminology, itself a recent addition to the discipline (Buist and Lenning 2016), is making to our understanding of the intersections of gender and crime. As it stands, many gender-responsive programmes which have been accepted by the state still bracket females together in ways which limit their personal expression and opportunities to limited categories of mother or carer and which place them in heterosexual relationships. Gender-responsive approaches were developed in a particular historical and geographical context and face the charge that they have also been built from a particular Western-centred viewpoint which might not be so easily transferred into different social and cultural contexts. As we have seen earlier, minority, Black and African feminists in particular have argued that their own realities differ in key ways from those which predominate in Western economies which have been shaped along a particular historical trajectory which is not mirrored outside the metropole. Ideas of women's empowerment, progression and civilisation have been interpreted differently as a consequence, with Western conceptions often serving to marginalise, ignore or even to further oppress women from different cultural and national backgrounds. As Lawston and Meiners (2014) recount, the history of well-intentioned interventions into women's imprisonment and sentencing has been dominated by the white middle-class philanthropist who has imposed their own ideals as to the standards which women should aspire to and be judged by. Reformers such as Bentham in the eighteenth and Elizabeth Fry in the nineteenth centuries were inherently paternalistic and patriarchal in their approach and goals to return female prisoners to respectability and to subservient, domesticated roles. While these early reformers strove to develop principles which would today be called 'woman-centred', their perceptions of women's needs were severely limited by their historical context and limited understanding of the lives of women who were subjected to sentencing, imprisonment and the rehabilitatory zeal of those who professed to have their interests at heart. Women of colour were not even considered within this early reformist framework and in the US continued to be incarcerated in separate wings of men's prisons while white women were more likely to be placed in all-female institutions (Freedman 1981 in Lawston and Meiners 2014).

It took the second-wave women's movement of the 1960s to inject a more complete understanding of women's oppression and its many facets. Simone de Beauvoir revealed the social construction of women as a deviant sex and bell hooks contributed an understanding of the oppression faced by the racialised female within society more generally and also within the feminist movement itself. Many feminists, however, still struggle with the implications of embracing a truly intersectional position. The current debate over the rights of women in Islam is a case in point. Many feminists in the secular West adopt very impassioned positions over the wearing of the burkha, hijab or burkinis, seeing the clothing adopted by some women in Islam as fundamentally symbolic of women's oppression, whilst many women of the Muslim faith who have adopted this clothing can still consider themselves as feminists and insist that theirs is a liberating and progressive political choice (Winter 2008). Neither 'side' of this debate has yet conceded to the other, revealing the fundamental separations that still exist between the perceptions of women from differing cultural backgrounds. It is impossible in these circumstances to suggest that there is one universal female experience, neither can there be one feminist standpoint which is accepted by all. Considering the complex ways in which gendered social relations are played out across the globe, using a term such as gender-responsive practice can prove to be fraught with difficulties and littered with potential sources of conflict.

Gender-responsive justice in an era of punitive sentencing

There exists considerable doubt as to whether gender-responsive justice can make much, or any, impact at all within the many penal systems across the world which have been affected by the late twentieth century's punitive turn. This return to punishment over welfare has been most marked across the Anglophone world where governments have clearly signalled their commitment to be 'tough on crime', but which can also be witnessed in the increasing numbers who are sentenced and imprisoned in many other countries which profess a more light-touch response to crime (Scraton 2015:188). The increasing severity of punishment has been accompanied by the warehousing of prisoners in larger institutions, and the tendency to treat those who come before the courts not as individuals with specific and varied needs but as members of a troublesome and increasingly violent group who must be contained and incapacitated for the protection of society more generally (Parenti 1999). Since the establishment in the West of the modern penal system based on utilitarian principles, and in older penal codes which predominate in many other countries, punishment has always maintained some deterrent function but there is evidence that in recent decades a number of governments across the globe have given their support to harsher sentencing climates in order to clearly signal to the general populace that the breaking of the law will be met with a tough response (Pratt and Eriksson 2013). As a result practices of punishment have shifted away from the resocialisation of the individual and towards more aggressive policies which have seen imprisonment more readily resorted to for those who have committed less serious crimes. At the same time this more punitive approach has led to the degradation of services offered to prisoners and the removal of prisoners' rights and more generally to a harsher climate facing all those who come before the attention of the courts.

The punitive turn in this retributive climate has hurt females to a greater extent than it has impacted upon males (Hedderman 2010). Women are more likely to be sentenced for those non-violent and less serious offences which have now been rendered prisonable. Once incarcerated, women feel the pains of imprisonment more deeply (Scraton 2016) and once again are doubly punished for what could be considered comparatively minor infractions. The increased tendency to hold women more severely to account for violations of the law has been played out during the same period of time that the call for gender-responsive justice has been made and more lately acted upon. Those who have studied the entire context in which women's sentencing and imprisonment take place have argued that gender-responsive justice has had little impact on penal systems where a 'retributive climate' (Scraton 2015) has taken precedence. As Hedderman (2010:490–491) has demonstrated, in Britain the judges and magistrates who are responsible for sentencing decisions have not been able to make their decisions in an environment which is free of political interference and as a result the numbers of women subjected to the pains of imprisonment have continued to increase, negatively impacting on their wider families and communities as well as the women as individuals.

The principles of gender-responsive justice hold that community-based sentencing is more appropriate for women and the recommendation that prison should be considered only as a last resort is a key element to their strategy. The evidence strongly suggests, however, that more extensive provision of community-based punishments has not impacted on sentencing decisions as judges and magistrates are already convinced that they only use prison where this is completely necessary and justified (Hedderman

2010). Consequently women face a continuing cycle of prison sentences which are too short for any attempt at rehabilitation to be made, not long enough for support services to be put in place on their re-entry into society, but which are harmful to family relationships, work commitments and housing retention. Women are then catapulted back into the desperate and impoverished conditions which they previously faced, without ongoing support, and these are precisely the conditions which are likely to increase the pressures upon them to break the law once more. Clearly a more fundamental shift in attitudes and practices is needed before harsh and retributive sentencing practices which have become embedded into systems of justice are abandoned in favour of more welfare-oriented and gender-sensitive decision-making.

The failure of gender-responsive justice models to make much headway in turning around the tide of aggressive and highly punitive sentencing criteria has led some commentators to suggest that a more fundamental rethinking of systems of justice is required to protect women from harmful practices. Prison abolitionists have been vocal in their criticism of gender-responsive approaches which suggest that the imprisonment of women could be better performed. The fact of incarceration and separation, they argue, is so damaging to women that improved conditions while imprisoned cannot begin to touch the problems women face inside prison walls. There they are subject to rules, regulations and authority which strip them of any control and agency. The carceral setting, they argue, cannot relieve women of responsibility and care or provide them with an opportunity to reflect on their actions, instead it takes away their ability to offer care, love and support to those for whom they feel responsible and as a consequence many women feel bereft and isolated, almost hollowed out as individuals and mere shells of the people that they have considered themselves to be and which allow their self-definition as 'good' women (Carlen 1983). Under these conditions women cannot heal or begin to 'make good' and to see their lives differently. Instead incarceration perpetuates the structural violence which women face, labels women as 'offenders' in their own eyes and the minds of others and takes away their agency and control. Many therefore see attempts to make prison 'women-friendly' as a contradiction in terms and propose abolition of imprisonment as the only way forward (Kilroy et al. 2013). More than the harms of imprisonment, however, the entire narrative of punishment can be considered as an injustice to so many women whose law-breaking is so intimately connected to the harms which they have experienced outside the legal system. As Scraton (2015) so powerfully shows, the systems of justice which prevail in any given society are inextricably linked to historical, political, ideological and cultural contexts. As these critics have demonstrated, rather than acting as a check and balance on inequities and the prejudices of legal and judicial systems, gender-responsive programmes themselves can often unfortunately reflect them.

References

Alfred, M.V. and Chlup, D.T. (2009) 'Neoliberalism, illiteracy, and poverty: framing the rise in black women's incarceration', *The Western Journal of Black Studies*, 33(4): 240–249.

Buist, C. and Lenning, E. (2016) *Queer Criminology*. London: Routledge.

Carlen, P. (1983) *Women's Imprisonment: A Study in Social Control*. London: Routledge and Kegan Paul.

Carlen, P. (2002) (ed) *Women and Punishment: The Struggle for Justice*. Cullompton: Willan.

Easton, H., Silvestri, M., Evans, K., Mathews, R. and Walklate, S. (2010) *Evaluation of the Conditional Cautioning Scheme with Referral to Together Women Project Women's Centres*. London: Ministry of Justice.

Gelsthorpe, L. (2013) 'Legitimacy, law and locality: making the case for change', in Malloch, M. and McIvor, G. (eds), *Women, Punishment and Social Justice: Human Rights and Penal Practices*. London: Routledge, pp. 13–24.

Gordoliza, R.P. (2013) 'Tracking the invisible: young Gitana women and punishment in Anadalusia', in Malloch, M. and McIvor, G. (eds), *Women, Punishment and Social Justice. Human rights and penal practices*. London: Routledge, pp. 178–194.

Gregory, J. (1986) 'Sex, class and crime: towards a non-sexist criminology', in Matthews, R. (ed), *Confronting Crime*. London: Routledge, pp. 53–71.

Hall, M.T., Golder, S., Conley, C.L. and Sawning, S. (2011) 'Designing programming and interventions for women in the criminal justice system', *American Journal of Criminal Justice*, 38(1): 27–50.

Hannah-Moffat, K. (2002) 'Creating choices: reflecting on choices', in Carlen, P. (ed), *Women and Punishment: The Struggle for Justice*. Cullompton: Willan, pp. 199–219.

Hannah-Moffat, K. (2008) 'Re-imaging gendered penalties: the myth of gender-responsivity', in Carlen, P., *Imaginary Penalities*. Cullompton: Willan, pp. 193–217.

Hannah-Moffat, K. (2010) 'Sacrosanct or flawed: risk, accountability and gender-responsive penal politics', *Current Issues in Criminal Justice*, 22(2): 193–215.

Hedderman, C. (2010) 'Government policy on women offenders: Labour's legacy and the coalition's challenge', *Punishment and Society*, 12(4): 485–500.

Hudson, B. (2002) 'Balancing rights and risks: dilemmas of justice and difference', in Gray, N.S., Laing, J.M. and Noaks, L. (eds), *Criminal Justice, Mental Health and the Politics of Risk*. London: Cavendish, pp. 99–122.

Kegan Gardiner, J. (2005) 'Men, masculinities, and feminist theory', in Kimmel, M.S., Hearn, J. and Connell, R.W. (eds), *Handbook of Studies on Men and Masculinities*. London: Sage, pp. 35–50.

Kendall, K. (2002) 'Time to think again about cognitive behavioural programmes', in Carlen, P. (ed), *Women and Punishment: The Struggle for Justice*. Cullompton: Willan, pp. 182–198.

Kendall, K. and Pollack, S. (2005) 'Taming the shrew: regulating prisoners through women-centred mental health programming', *Critical Criminology*, 13(1): 71–87.

Kilroy, D., Barton, P., Quixley, S., George, A. and Russell, E. (2013) 'Decentring the prison: abolitionist approaches to working with criminalized women', in Carlton, B. and Segrave, M. (eds), *Women Exiting Prison: Critical Essays on Gender, Post-Release Support and Survival*. London: Routledge, pp. 156–180.

Lawston, J. (2013) 'Prisons, gender responsive strategies and community sanctions: the expansion of punishment in the United States', in Malloch, M. and McIvor, G. (eds), *Women, Punishment and Social Justice: Human Rights and Penal Practices*. Abingdon: Routledge, pp. 109–120.

Lawston, J. and Meiners, E.R. (2014) 'Ending our expertise: feminists, scholarship, and prison abolition', *Feminist Formations*, 26(2): 1–25.

Mauer, M. and Chesney-Lind, M. (2002) 'Invisible punishment: the collateral consequences of mass imprisonment', www.sentencingproject.org/publications/invisible-punishment-the-collateral-consequences-of-mass-imprisonment/ [Accessed 15 July 2014].

Mills, L., Barocas, B., and Ariel, B. (2013) 'The next generation of court-mandated domestic violence treatment: a comparison study of batterer intervention and restorative justice programs', *Journal of Experimental Criminology*, 9(1): 65–90.

Morash, M. (2010) *Women on Probation and Parole: A Feminist Critique of Community Programs and Services*. Boston, MA: Northeastern University Press.

Parenti, C. (1999) *Lockdown America: Police and Prisons in the Age of Crisis*. London: Verso.

Poteat, S. (2002) 'The women at risk programme', in Carlen, P. (ed), *Women and Punishment: The Struggle for Justice*. Cullompton: Willan, pp. 125–137.

Pratt, J. and Eriksson, A. (2013) *Contrasts in Punishment: An Explanation of Anglophone Excess and Nordic Exceptionalism*. London: Routledge.

Scraton, P. (2015) 'Prisons and imprisonment in Northern Ireland', in McAlinden, A.-M. and Dwyer, C. (eds), *Criminal Justice in Transition: The Northern Ireland Context*. Oxford: Bloomsbury Academic, pp. 185–208.

Scraton, P. (2016) 'Bearing witness to the "pain of others": researching power, violence and resistance in a women's prison', *International Journal for Crime, Justice and Social Democracy*, 5(1): 5–20.

Sheehan, R. (2013) 'Justice and community for women in transition in Victoria, Australia', in Malloch, M. and McIvor, G. (eds), *Women, Punishment and Social Justice: Human Rights and Penal Practices*. London: Routledge, pp. 121–135.

Silvestri, M. and Crowther-Dowey, C. (2016) *Gender and Crime: A Human Rights Approach*. London: Sage.

Stark, J. (2015) 'Call yourself a woman? Feminists take on transgender community in bitter debate', *Sydney Morning Herald*, www.smh.com.au/national/what-makes-a-woman-feminists-take-on-transgender-community-in-bitter-debate-20151113-gkyk6u.html [Accessed 13 January 2016].

The National Re-entry Resource Centre (2012) 'Women engaged in the criminal justice system', www.youtube.com/watch?v=kcU4IF5-sQM [Accessed 16 March 2016].

The Sentencing Project (2015) 'Fact sheet: incarcerated women and girls', www.sentencingproject.org/wp-content/uploads/2016/02/Incarcerated-Women-and-Girls.pdf [Accessed 14 February 2016].

United Nations Office on Drugs and Crime (2014) *Handbook on Women and Imprisonment*. New York: United Nations, www.unodc.org/documents/justice-and-prison-reform/women_and_imprisonment_-_2nd_edition.pdf [Accessed 15 February 2016].

Winter, B. (2008) *Hijab & the Republic: Uncovering the French Headscarf Debate*. Syracuse, NY: Syracuse University Press.

Chapter 6

Gender-responsive justice

Feminism and resistance

The arguments which have been made to underpin the development of woman-centred, gender-specific and gender-responsive justice have been developed over a number of decades and have changed in their emphasis and tone during this period. Beginning in the 1970s the argument for women-centred justice was informed by feminist concerns that women had been written out of the discipline and needed to be placed at the centre of discussion in order that the different needs of women and girls could be met but also so that criminological theories could be reconsidered and reframed to take into account the experiences of the female sex. This argument was soon reformulated by feminist criminologists as a concern with gendered social relationships and their impact – initially on women and girls, then subsequently on men as the problematisation of masculinity was brought into the field of criminological debate. The proponents of gender-specific justice raised important questions concerning the ways in which women were treated within the criminal justice system and revealed current systems of justice to be gender-blind and harmful to women and girls. The subsequent call for a gender-responsive justice utilised the knowledge which had been generated by woman-centred and gender-specific perspectives to more closely interrogate the workings of the criminal justice system and to challenge the risk-centred, masculinist logics which were driving criminal justice and penal practices at the turn of the century.

The shifting focus

When feminist methods and logics were employed to understand the law-breaking behaviour of women and girls the focus was initially on understanding women, their motivations and the circumstances of their involvement in the commission of crime but then moved towards a critique of systems of criminal justice, punishment and imprisonment and the ways in which these discriminated against members of the female sex. As the focus has moved away from understanding women's lives more generally and become an examination and critique of systems of criminal justice, the focus of attention has narrowed and become much more clearly criminological than sociological. In a sense then the study moved from one which was woman-centred to one which became system-centred, albeit that the concern was to ensure that such systems became more 'female-friendly' and gender-aware. Subsequently arguments were raised as to how systems of criminal justice might be reconstructed in such a way as to avoid further harming those women who came to their attention. The study of gender-responsive justice has consequently become more of a reformist project, working within the parameters of the existing systems which have already been set by criminal justice practice and policy constructed using masculinist systems of knowledge and logic. As we have entered a period of penal populism and a subsequent hardening of attitudes towards 'the offender' there has been much to do in order to ensure that women and girls are spared the worst excesses of the system and that criminal justice professionals and policy-makers retain some kind of empathy towards those who are brought into the courts and prison systems. This shift is therefore understandable but it brings with it its own dangers.

In their desire to impact on and improve existing practice, proposals for gender-responsive programmes have to a large extent incorporated the individualisation of the problem of crime and law-breaking behaviour which is a feature of existing systems. Consequently gender-responsive interventions have looked to develop and instigate better ways to alter the behaviour patterns of individual women and to empower and enable them in ways that they may find tap into their own personal reserves of strength and resilience. This approach involves the adoption of a kinder and more understanding methodology of working with women who break the law, and it is one which individual women appear to prefer and to respond to, but it nevertheless is limited in its particular scope (Hedderman, Palmer and Hollin 2008). Whether programmes utilising gender-responsive approaches are more effective in terms of reducing women's law-breaking remains a moot point, with evaluations providing mixed results. However, even to ask this question imposes masculinist logics on an area which it was previously argued should be feminised and concerned with shifting the discourse away from its narrow concern with crime and towards an understanding of the entirety of women's experiences and the gendered circumstances within which their opportunities and potential are severely constrained.

Understanding transgression

As long ago as 1988 Maureen Cain, in an address to the American Society of Criminology on the occasion of her acceptance of the Sellin Glueck Award, argued that the boundaries of criminology were too narrowly focused and that the discipline was unable to fully understand the circumstances surrounding the law-breaking of women and girls (Cain 1990). She argued that criminology and its focus on criminality had to be 'transgressed' and that the discipline and its main precepts should be deconstructed and built again (reconstructed) as a very different sort of enterprise. What the discipline's narrow focus on crime and criminality had entirely missed, she argued, was that the problem of crime is actually a problem of social control. The interventions of early feminist criminologists had been able to reveal this glaring lack of insight by 'taking the question of what women really do out of the straight-jacket of defining their relevant doings solely in offence terms' (Cain 1990:4) and by exploring instead the complete relationship of women and girls to crime and criminality. Once the female experience was placed centre-stage a very different narrative began to emerge. The replacement of the male gaze by one informed by a female perspective revealed that the problems which women and girls encounter both outside and inside systems of criminal justice are all related to gendered social control mechanisms. Their patterns of victimisation, of law-breaking and their treatment at the hands of the criminal justice system were all shaped by the same societal controls and stereotypes which predominate as to 'appropriate' behaviours for the female sex and by the structural inequalities of patriarchy which handed the power of control to men and boys. This female gaze also raised a key question which had hitherto been ignored concerning the overwhelming maleness of criminality. What is it, these feminist criminologists asked, about men and their masculinity which makes this sex so prone to criminality and so likely to choose women as their victims (Naffine 1990)? Again the answer for Cain did not rely on the study of patterns of crime but instead lay in studying the mechanisms and patterns of gendered social control.

The necessary reconstruction of criminology could only take place, Cain argued, after a period in which existing paradigms which shaped the subject were fully investigated and their true nature exposed. The first key element of extant theories which feminist criminologists exposed was their masculinist character as centred on and informed by the male experience alone. This in itself revealed the partial and male-centred nature of the subject which had all but ignored half of the global population. In addition, however, when criminologists, who were at that point overwhelmingly male, had considered women's experiences they had considered women as they had considered men before them, as though the female sex had recourse to the same opportunities and were afforded the same agency as the male. This masculinist gaze could not see the oppression of women and therefore, on the rare occasions when women were studied, criminologists utilised an extremely distorted logic to try to explain why women might break the law (Gregory 1986). At the first awakening of second-wave feminism and the birth of the women's liberation movement at the end of the 1960s this same logic, this time spoken by a female criminologist, declared women to have achieved the liberty to act just like men and to be well on the way to achieving the same levels of criminality (Adler 1975). The victimisation of women, its nature and extent remained absent from the discussion and masculinist logics were utilised to attack the progress of women and girls.

When feminist criminologists turned towards the study of gender and its impacts rather than merely studying women and comparing their experiences to those of men, the masculinist nature of criminology was exposed on another level. Women's victimisation at the hands of men and boys was revealed to be of staggering proportions. The study of domestic violence, sexual assault, rape and intimate partner abuse inspired a new critique of systems of law which had institutionalised male control over the female sex for centuries. The law itself and the institutions which supported it were exposed as 'man-made' (Naffine 1990), highly gendered and unable to protect women and girls from gendered patterns of victimisation. Feminist scholars of jurisprudence and legal practitioners in some countries were successful in overturning the worst of the laws which overtly reinforced the oppression of the female sex so that women and girls might begin to feel that they had equal recourse to the law when victimised. This replacement of anti-female and discriminatory laws with those which recognise the female as a subject in her own right and as equally entitled to the protection of the law has been a remarkable achievement but there is still much to be done. This critique and partial reshaping of the law has not succeeded in deconstructing existing legal paradigms or in reconstructing them along feminist lines as Cain suggested was the ultimate project, although it has made some inroads into the removal of some significant oppressive practices.

Another area where the gender perspective made a significant contribution within criminology was in inspiring a new area of exploration on the links between masculinity and crime. The 1990s saw an explosion of interest in the study of the male as a gendered subject who is also constrained in behaviour by limitations imposed by social constructions of masculinity. Work carried out on the gendered male revealed the significance to criminology of 'hegemonic masculinity' which reifies the male as the dominator in economic, social and sexual relationships (Connell 1995). This 'ideal type' or form of masculinity is revered above others and celebrates the domination of the white, male heterosexual over other types of 'subordinated' masculinity. The work of male and female criminologists heavily influenced by feminist theory was cognisant of the different ways in which men could 'perform' their gender (Messerschmidt 1997). These theorists explored the ways in which expressions of masculinity impacted on the decision-making of men and boys. Their work did not, however, suggest that there was an equivalence between the many constraints imposed on women and girls as a result of their gendered oppression and the constraints both psychological and social which impacted on male behaviour (Kimmel, Hearn and Connell 2005). Their work was much more nuanced and subtle, it reflected on the dominant positions occupied by males at one and the same time as it discussed the ways in which men and boys could be shaped and damaged by the heteronormative expectations of an ascendant, white masculinity and the expectations of privilege which could be gained from 'signing up' to such a dominant construction of self.

Putting women centre-stage

Alongside the deconstruction of existing and male-centred criminological theorisations, Cain's transgressive project demanded that feminists adopt a fully reflexive approach to understanding the female condition. This approach, she suggested, must go beyond 'photographing the garbage can' (Cain 1990:7), that is, it must look beyond the manifest behaviours of women and girls to reveal the underlying, structural forces which have shaped and limited women's experiences and can therefore help to explain the decisions which they make. It is not enough, Cain argued, to look at what women do and to condemn that behaviour, whether that be manifested in living outside the bounds of law or accepted morality or that which appears to reinforce their gendered oppression or which even appears anathema to either the feminist or criminological project. Feminist criminologists must instead be prepared to reflect on why such behaviour appears to be a preferred option for many women and girls. It is also necessary to understand that real social advantages can accrue to females who behave in particular socially prescribed ways. As Cain explained:

> Working class girls are being entirely realistic when they recognise that their life chances are related to their ability to secure a good wage earner as a mate, and all women who do not couple will be vulnerable to systematic denigration of their life-style.
>
> (Cain 1990:8)

In these circumstances it can appear immediately beneficial and advantageous for their future progression if females adopt a normative femininity which ties them to passivity, to handing their agency over to significant males and which keeps them embedded within harmful and toxic relationships. Women and girls are taught, after all, that without men they are incomplete and incapable of many actions, so too many believe that there is no alternative but to endure what is bad in order to maintain what they consider they have achieved to the positive, whether that be a home, family, romantic love, practical support and so on. Included in a gendered perspective then is the requirement not to judge others but to attempt to see their situation through their eyes. In addition, real alternatives must be put in place which women can easily access and which allow them to live differently. Only then is it possible to begin to intervene positively in ways which can reveal to the woman herself that a different course of action is not only beneficial in the long term but is also possible in the immediate future.

The centrality of feminist praxis

The reconstruction of criminological theory, the law and criminal justice practices along alternative, women-centred and feminised lines is the necessary final element of the transgressive project. In contrast to the male-centred approaches of the past a woman-centred reconstruction should start not from the viewpoint of the detached expert and professional, but from below, from hearing the voices of women who are caught up in gendered systems of oppression. It is also a reconstructive project which is based on intervention and action and involves listening to and working alongside those women who are actively seeking ways to understand and to restructure social relationships in ways which seek to rebuild social organisations and relationships along egalitarian lines. It is alongside these women, and using their knowledge, that the essential understanding of gender itself would be either reconstructed or replaced, gendered social control mechanisms could be dis-established and the false opposition between male and female deconstructed in its entirety. What would replace the long-established systems of patriarchal control could not be fully known in the here and now but must be constructed in the struggle to overcome the old. As Cain has argued, the language of patriarchy is so fully embedded in the structures of society that a new discourse needs to be created in its stead. Before the second wave of feminism, she reminds us, society had no language with which to describe many of the different elements of women's oppression precisely because women's voices were isolated, marginalised and ignored. For a new understanding to emerge a new language must develop which can encompass consciousness of the multifaceted and deep-seated nature of oppression and this can only be achieved by women, with women and for women. It is a deeply feminist project which cannot be sidelined and overstepped and there are no shortcuts which can be taken.

The early feminists of the second-wave movement looked to understand and consolidate their knowledge through feminist praxis – the blending of theoretical insights with feminist activism so that both theory and activism benefited from each other. As has been outlined, the woman-centred knowledge which they sought to reveal and to bring centre-stage had to be discovered through the sharing of the female experience, raising consciousness as to the true impact of patriarchal social structures and finding female-centred ways of intervening in the social world. This sharing of women's knowledge brought new ways of thinking and acting which had not been part of the male repertoire. Much of the early work conducted in the area of women's victimisation, for example, culminated in the development of protective, women-only spaces in which women and children could escape from domestic violence, gain support from other women and begin to heal. The women's refuge movement was one such response to violence against women which was born out of a feminist praxis (Hanmer 2000). The actions of women who were prepared to work with others to make a positive difference had further significant impacts. It brought therapeutic interventions to the forefront of work with women and girls and developed a new language which could be used to express the pains of physical and sexual violence and the resilience and strength of those who had lived through trauma who would henceforth be referred to as 'survivors' rather than merely victims. While these therapeutic and healing spaces were not the total havens which might have been initially envisaged, they represented a departure from existing practices and demonstrated a different and more positive way forward. Feminist interventions achieved a significant impact outside of the female-centred provision which they offered and suggested a better way of working with all survivors of trauma which recognised the importance of talking, sharing experiences with other survivors and the general effectiveness of therapeutic intervention. The victim's movement worldwide grew from these early interventions and positively affected services offered to both men and women (Walklate 2006).

In a number of ways then, the impact of feminist praxis was generalised and absorbed into best practice across a whole range of social interventions. It is important to acknowledge however that second-wave feminism was never a uniform movement with a universally agreed programme for reform (Hanmer 2000). From the outset many feminists identified with a specific feminist standpoint – whether liberal, radical, socialist or even revolutionary Marxist (Walklate 1995). Each took a different theoretical position on the origins of women's oppression and consequently followed a different path to its elimination. Poststructuralist feminism followed Cain's example by looking to expose and deconstruct the masculinist mono-logic reasoning of law and criminology and to bring in the recognition of different subjectivities within the feminist project (Carrington 2002). Black, third-world and postmodern feminism standpoints subsequently questioned the assumptions of the women's movement and the concept of the 'sisterhood' of all women, suggesting that the lived experiences of women were so varied as to make the unified appeal to 'womanhood' a meaningless pursuit (Carrington 2002). Notwithstanding this 'fragmentation' of second-wave feminism, 'women-centred' activism continued to make its impact felt for many years to come.

The absorption of feminism into mainstream practice

In the UK and Canada the promotion of substantive equality and support for the adoption of equal opportunities legislation transformed central and local government agendas in the 1980s and early 1990s, opening up the labour market to a new generation of female practitioners and professionals who consequently brought alternative perspectives into the management and provision of many services (Segal 1989). Segal (1989) reflects on the entry of women into the labour movement in the UK during this period, which was considered an important element to the feminisation of the workplace even though socialist feminists did not entirely trust male-dominated institutions. The feminisation of service delivery however was achieved, not just through an increase in the numbers of women entering the professions, but predicated on promotion and adoption of policy and practice which was informed by particular forms of feminist praxis and which set a challenge to existing institutional directives. In addition, socialist feminists active within the early women's liberation movement of the 1970s argued that women should pursue feminist and women-centred agendas inside trade unions to further cement an equalities agenda in employment practices. Female trade unionists were often shouted down or belittled in the process of making their arguments but nevertheless, Segal argued, they began to make substantial inroads into male-dominated ways of thinking. So much so that in 1979 the national trades union body in England and Wales (the Trades Union Congress) sponsored a historic national march for abortion rights which took place in the centre of the political establishment, marching to Westminster, London. The gains which women trade union activists made were hard-won but were nevertheless significant steps 'concerned with transforming the politics and power relations of everyday life' (Segal 1989:14) and feminist trade unionists therefore sought to change systems and practices for all. The replacement of masculinist approaches and frameworks, it was argued, would improve extant circumstances for women and men, removing some of the worst constraints of a systemic discrimination for women and marginalised others but also in helping to rethink and reconstruct the ideals of masculinity and therefore ultimately benefiting men in the process.

As Segal (1989:14) outlines, feminist activists encountered an 'extraordinary difficulty [...] confronting men's cultural and social dominance'. The power held by men was not given up easily. Feminists encountered discriminatory social attitudes which held back their progress and barriers were put in their way by men protecting normative masculine ideals and arguing that certain areas should remain the preserve of males. In addition the social structures which underpinned male dominance and power could remain intact even as discrimination was made illegal and as the boundaries of masculinity were moved to some extent. Shifts in social attitudes and the opening up of employment and professional practice to women, therefore, did not necessarily lead to a wholesale transformation in the mechanisms of social power. Indeed it has been argued that as social attitudes appeared to open up and to begin to question and erode white male privilege, the former bastions of male power began to organise to protect their power-base. One aspect of this regrouping was the success of the politics of anti-feminist backlash but perhaps more subtly their promotion of the idea that feminism had won the battle of the sexes and was consequently no longer a necessary arena of struggle began to have an effect. The 'women-centred' principles of the early second-wave feminism were consequently considered by some as antiquated and no longer needed in the post-feminist world (Faludi 1991). Ironically the success of feminist praxis in bringing women into the centre-stage and challenging the supremacy of the male in public life was taken as a sign that feminist struggle could subsequently be put aside.

For socialist feminists such as Segal, however, the moment in which the women's movement appeared to have reached a successful conclusion should have been seen as merely the beginning of a revolution which had to be pushed forward in other arenas and in other regions of the world. The intervention of third-world, black, lesbian and transgender feminists among others demonstrated the need to take the discourse and practices which had been developed and championed by women-centred praxis in the West into new arenas. As we have seen in preceding chapters, this call to internationalise feminist theory and practice was taken up through the development of UN policy-making, a move which has been heralded as the feminising of human rights discourses (Barbaret 2014). In individual countries too women's movements played their part in democratising and liberalising anti-democratic regimes and linked up with similar movements worldwide to ensure that real changes in the perception and treatment of women were achieved (Carrington 2015). As women gained a voice in government and policy-making their activism inevitably changed its form and character so that:

> strategies changed from resistance to working within and alongside the United Nations and the state to form NGOs [non-governmental organisations] to bring about positive changes to the lives of women and children.
>
> (Carrington 2015:90)

This incorporation of feminist ideas into the mainstream has been dubbed *femocratisation* in the West and *institutionalizadas* in Latin America (Carrington 2015). Femocracies are created where 'feminists are able to create a power-base inside state institutions' (Gregory and Lees 1994:81). Their influence can be seen in the many interventions which the UN has made in feminising its work in developing countries and in its policy of gender mainstreaming. Femocratisation represents a point at which the goals of liberal feminists are accepted by state institutions and non-government agencies alike, which together form alliances in order to change the policy landscape. The practices of working with women change as a consequence, as do the aims and objectives of the policies which are actioned. The concern is that feminists engaged within such bureaucracies move their agenda forwards without 'selling out' and without severing their links with the grassroots of feminism and feminist activism (Gregory and Lees 1994:81).

The femocratisation of the feminist project is welcomed by many but has its critics. Nancy Fraser (2009) has argued that there have been many unintended consequences of this shift from grassroots activism to working to influence large-scale bureaucracies from the inside. It has, she argued, led to a legitimation of neoliberal perspectives on both the state and the economy, demanding women's entry into employment but on terms which have kept women in low-paid and low-status jobs, legitimating the marketisation and privatisation of services and enabling the retrenchment of the state. The femocracy has championed micro-businesses run by women as offering a solution to their individual economic circumstances even as they have replaced better-paid and sustained employment opportunities and contributed to what Carlen has termed the feminisation of poverty worldwide. What Fraser calls the NGO-ification of feminist activism has, she believes, reduced the ability of femocrats to criticise capitalism and 'its gender-based distributive injustices' (Funk 2013:187) as their work has become dependent on the largesse of neoliberal institutions for continued funding. In fact neoliberalism, Fraser argues, has successfully co-opted feminist arguments to legitimate fundamentally exploitative practices, as it has done with many other progressive movements. Funk sees in femocratisation an inevitable depoliticisation and deradicalisation of feminist politics which have conceded to the argument that femocrats working to a neoliberalist agenda can offer a revolutionary and community-based alternative to the androcentrism of state and legislature.

Femocratisation, gender-responsive justice and unintended consequences

Second-wave feminism, Fraser (2009) argues, has become fully co-opted into the neoliberal project. Women's problems have been individualised and policy and practices have been divorced from the radical political perspectives and connections to the labour movement which were developed in the 1970s and 1980s. Instead alliances have been made with neoliberal governance structures and institutions which have used their 'statecraft' to impose the logics of the market onto popular discourse and to submit organisations to what Vivek Chibber (2016:12) has referred to as 'the dull compulsion of economic relations'. In order to achieve some modicum of stability and to access ongoing funding, organisations thereby submit, generally in an unconscious way, to practices and ideologies which run counter to their own fundamental principles and interests. Furthermore the bureaucratic institutions which are in control of funding and the policy process allow ideas which appear to run counter to the imperatives of capital to be accommodated at various times but these alternative perspectives can never be fully embraced and brought into the mainstream because they ultimately threaten the basis upon which capital builds and sustains itself. At the heart of the current system are distinction, division, inequality and hierarchy and principles such as compassion, empathy, inclusion and self-governance remain antithetical to the project of capital.

In the sphere of criminal justice this femocratisation of policy has provided many examples of work which is designed to take women and girls' needs into consideration as victims and law-breakers. It can be seen in the promotion and development of specialised services for female victims, in the many projects which have included gender-responsive programmes for women and girls and it has even resulted in the provision of women-only police stations in Latin America and in India and Bangladesh (Lee and Haider 2012). It has seen the modification of laws so that they reflect the experiences of the female sex and changes in policy in too many areas to recount here. It is what lay behind the Canadian state's change in policy towards female law-breakers in the 1990s. As we have seen in previous chapters a 'femocracy' within the UN has also led to the international adoption of more women-friendly standards and guidelines for dealing with women who have broken the law and which have set new principles to ensure that the human rights of women are assured even as they are punished and incarcerated by adopting methods and practices which are cognisant of gender-responsive principles.

Nevertheless, the incorporation of gender-responsive principles into state and transnational bureaucracies has led to some unintended consequences. High among these is the depoliticisation and deradicalisation of policy agendas which Funk (2013) outlined as an almost inevitable outcome of the integration of feminist activism into systems of power and control. This is a particular danger when seeking to alter the workings of the criminal justice system which is after all built on the fundamental principles and practices of disempowerment and control. Any expectations that this system can be reformed have often been dashed. In Latin America, Carrington argues, women's police stations have been shown to have fallen far short of their intended outcomes; female police officers have retained the masculinist assumptions which lie at the very core of their craft and profession and have remained largely unsympathetic to the plight of women who are unable to leave violent relationships (Carrington 2015). The idea that prisons could become therapeutic and reintegrative spaces has proved equally problematic and as Hannah-Moffat (2008:214) has written, 'the history of penal reform confirms that correctional institutions have the ability to absorb, integrate and temporarily silence critical discourses.' In the UK, Hedderman (2010) observes, the legislature has only ever increased the severity of sentencing and never reduced it (492).

There are fundamental contradictions between the principles of 'woman-centred' policy and the ways in which punishment has been conceptualised and practised. In the current context of penal populism the contradictions are all too obvious yet gender-responsive programmes are still attempted. The environment in which gender-responsive programmes are inserted cannot be ignored and the impact of environments which are not conducive to feminist progress should be acknowledged. Covington, an early champion of gender-specific and gender-responsive programmes, has reflected on the difficulties of sustaining this work in the current climate. She has highlighted such threats as a continued punitive culture, a lack of resources, the absence of supportive work environments for staff who suffer burn-out as a consequence and cuts to public services which mean that services can only be accessed in dilapidated and unsafe spaces (White 2014). In the UK a shift in penal philosophy has meant that public sector agencies are required to adopt private sector managerial principles (Clarke 2004:16) led by a results-oriented culture. The individual autonomy of staff and their previous commitment to a culture of care have been replaced by a culture of public protection and risk management in order that they can demonstrate that they meet economy, efficiency and effectiveness targets. In too many projects which claim to be gender-aware, a culture of punishment prevails with staff expected to report their clients for non-attendance, for example, thereby effectively punishing women who are not able or ready to engage in what can be difficult and challenging work (Clarke 2004, Hannah-Moffat 2002, Easton et al. 2010). In addition there is the problem of providing ongoing support for women who have used these services, which is in reality largely absent, so that once the programmes are completed the safety nets for women disappear (Clarke 2004:19). Covington has also raised the problem of organisations which purchase 'off-the-shelf' programmes without considering the culture and environment in which the services are run. As she explains:

> I think everyone's on the bandwagon for trauma-informed services, but most people think that means picking up a curriculum and running a group versus really looking at the culture of your program.
>
> (White 2014:9)

As Covington's observations reveal, the cultural environment in which gender-responsive programmes are run is crucial to their intended outcomes. This culture has to be a positive environment for its staff as much as its service-users, offering good jobs in sustainable services which are situated in appropriate, secure and comfortable spaces. Too often many of these elements are absent.

Gender-responsive programmes, women and desistance

The funding of many gender-responsive programmes, then, has been tied to the imperatives of the state and they are assessed and evaluated through the lens of desistance outcomes. However, a brief look at the literature demonstrates that there is still so much that we do not know about the best way of working with women who break the law. Daly's pathways to crime analysis helped to explain the particular circumstances in which women's law-breaking takes place and to reveal the gendered nature of that behaviour but looking at pathways to crime gives us only a partial picture. Mainstream criminology has been concerned with the aetiology of law-breaking behaviour because it hopes to contribute to the lessening of actions which are deemed to be socially problematic and harmful. It is suggested that there is a direct link between individual change and a positive outcome for society and in addition that there is a clear link between the motivation to commit a crime and the decision-making around when to quit. This does not consider that motivations to change may be high but structural circumstances do not allow it. Mainstream criminology has had very little to say about women's desistance and knows very little about the experiences that women go through before, during and after they break the law. There are few examples of desistance theory which are based around the female experience and services developed within the criminal justice system have rarely addressed women as a category worthy of particular consideration. There has been 'very little research in relation to effective practices in the supervision of female offenders' (Trotter 2007:135). Theories which have been developed to understand desistance have been based on studies which have not traditionally included females as their subjects and they speak to the experiences of men and boys only.

The oldest and most influential explanation of desistance is maturational reform theory which suggests that most offenders will simply grow up and grow away from anti-social and criminal behaviour (Glueck and Glueck 1940, Farrington 1997). Social bonds theory suggests that law-breaking behaviour is linked to weak social bonding and that building strong ties to family, relationships and the world of work will result in a weaker commitment to the commission of crime. More recently research has suggested that the individual's particular narrative of self is key to both their criminality and their desistance from crime (Burnett 1992). This narrative perspective suggests that desistance occurs as a result of subjective changes in a person's sense of self and identity and can lead to a 'moment of change' after which the individual reorients himself (for these theories too are largely based on the male experience) and is able to make different life-choices (Maruna 2000). Research has also been conducted on 'assisted desistance', exploring the ways in which those working with the individual offender can best support them to make and sustain necessary lifestyle changes (Rex 1999, Farrall 2002). These latter studies have concluded that desistance is a complex process which involves a multiplicity of factors, not just pertaining to the individual's personal circumstances, age, relationships, narratives and professional support but also to the community, social and personal contexts in which either persistence in or desistance from law-breaking takes place. The applicability of these theoretical frameworks to the choices made by women and girls is, however, unknown.

What do women tell us?

Criminologists who have focused on women and girls have raised a number of questions relating to the generalisability of desistance theories to the decision-making of girls and women. They have pointed out the flaws in existing theories and their gender-blindness. Maturational reform theory, for example, has not taken into consideration that girls begin, and end, their law-breaking behaviour a number of years earlier than do boys. It has nothing to say either about the persistence of certain types of crimes which are committed by men against women in domestic and intimate relationships. There is little evidence to suggest that men desist from domestic violence, coercive control and sexual abuse as they mature, indeed the opposite may be true in that maturation and entering into intimate relationships with women increases their opportunity to commit such crimes. Social bonds theory also ignores this particular arena of male crime which may increase precisely as intimate and domestic relationships are formed. It also makes no acknowledgement of research which demonstrates that women and girls can commit crime to escape the social controls and victimisation which they experience in patriarchal family and community structures (Gregory 1986).

When researchers talk to women themselves about their law-breaking they find that existing systems do not work effectively for women. Their research suggests that existing systems are too focused around the crime committed but that a greater emphasis should be put on alleviating the social circumstances that surround the decision-making of women who break the law. They counsel that early intervention in the lives of women who are struggling in a system in which so much is stacked against them is necessary and that this can put their lives on a better course which may mean that a crime is never committed (McIvor 2004). They argue for a strong base of community support and networks which can alleviate debt, deliver meaningful employment and training opportunities, give advice on managing relationships, empower women and girls to make different choices and increase their feelings of self-worth and self-esteem (Roberts 2010). Conversations with women who break the law also reveal that these women often show a marked willingness to work to change their lives and that they are willing to ask for support to help them to do this. Women will often exhibit strong feelings of guilt, shame and remorse and ask for understanding and empathy rather than judgement and stigmatisation. The label of offender is one which they wear heavily, one which can trap them in negative self-loathing and hold them back from future progression. Their lack of self-worth needs to be sensitively addressed and this is often best done in supportive women-only environments where each woman's individual achievements are recognised and confirmed (Hedderman, Palmer and Hollin 2008). Women also tell researchers that they need people to talk to who will believe in them, will listen to them and not talk at them, that they need people who will not judge their past behaviour but will help them to move forward in a positive direction and that they need to be given time to reappraise themselves, see their own value and be given respite from the difficulties in their lives and from their caring responsibilities in order that they can rediscover who they are and where their strengths lie (Easton et al. 2010, Radcliffe and Hunter 2016).

More recent conversations with women who have been sentenced also suggest that the point at which women begin their process through the criminal justice system represents a point of significant rupture in the individual woman's sense of self-identity. Criminality is not associated with the female experience and to be arrested, tried, sentenced and imprisoned places women in spaces which are heavily masculinised and in which they have no place. The entry of women and girls into such environments is a 'catastrophic' moment for women which strips them of their femininity, their womanhood and their place in the world and places them in a context in which they are stripped of meaning and direction (Williams, Green and Williams 2017). Within these spaces there is no blueprint for 'the good [female] convict' and, as Williams and colleagues remind us, there are no accepted 'rules' or known strategies which the individual woman can abide by in order to aid her survival. She is subjected, however, to a plethora of petty restrictions, degradations and humiliations designed to render her body even more docile and compliant and therefore highly vulnerable (Scraton 2016). There is no respite in the criminal justice system from the physical and psychological pressures and discriminations which women and girls face 'on the outside', only an intensification of the same.

The enduring and exceptional pains of imprisonment faced by women and girls who are institutionalised and incarcerated have led a number of scholars to argue that the feminist position should be one which foregrounds an abolitionist stance and that to work to 'improve' conditions for women and girls in prison or in the sentencing process merely traps them into a system which is in reality incapable of reform and which needs to be totally deconstructed (Carlton and Segrave 2013). Yet the adoption of gender-responsive programmes and principles may have the opposite effect. Lawston and Meiners (2014) use the example of Dwight Prison in Illinois to illustrate this problem. Despite being condemned for its poor facilities the prison was kept open because it provided sexual assault services for women. Prison reform organisations therefore utilised feminist and gender scholarship to ensure its continued existence. As Lawston and Meiners remark, 'gender responsive prisons and initiatives often expand and strengthen the prison system' and they ask whether 'Once the gender-responsive prison is opened will it ever be shut?' (Lawston and Meiners 2014:4). Utilising Cain's transgressive strategies and placing women's voices and experiences at the centre of scholarship confirms the abolitionist position as an important and 'woman-centred' stance for feminist scholars and activists to take, but it is one which is unfortunately not currently at the forefront of our attention.

Feminism as a critical endeavour

As many feminists working within criminology have remarked, taking a feminist stance is about so much more than adding women to the mix of available knowledge and practice. It is a critical endeavour which demands transformational change in society. However, in a period which has become obsessed with criminal justice outcomes and the *What Works?* agenda, a key area which gender-responsive practitioners, policy-makers and theorists have had to engage with is the question of desistance from crime – what can be done to ensure that women and girls disengage from law-breaking and adopt more pro-social behaviours. As a consequence much of the debate in practice has become more focused around what is effective in reforming the individual female. This approach is too far from that which sees the vulnerable situation of women and girls as a structural violence which must be addressed but locates the vulnerability within the individual woman. Of course structural vulnerability is experienced as a personal issue but it cannot be removed through individual action. Its removal needs a collective response and action.

The call for a woman-wise penology which could reinvent and replace androcentric, masculinist and ultimately patriarchal punishment practices and 'justice' systems has been somewhat overshadowed by a more narrowly defined concern to ensure that women's voices are heard, their experiences taken into account and their needs acknowledged (Carlen 1989). The more radical, revolutionary and transformative edge of much early feminist theorising which required a fundamental challenge to masculinist powers and privileges has been lost in the process. So has the analysis of penality which is firmly undertaken as a critique of gendered social control in society more generally. As Laureen Snider (1998) so cogently articulated 20 years ago:

> feminists working in the fields of criminology and law have long acknowledged that deep-seated social problems such as domestic assault can only be ameliorated by ideological and structural change, the very time-consuming and laborious process now being pushed into the background by policies of criminalization.
>
> (2)

The irony, Snider explains, is that too many feminists working both outside and within criminology who see themselves as progressive interventionists have fallen behind the argument that the criminalisation and punishment of transgressors is key to building safer societies. However, this logic is dangerous and leads, she argues, to the creation of more violence and misogyny and does nothing to challenge and reverse structural violence against the female sex. Indeed women have been caught up in this agenda of criminalisation to such an extent that their incarceration is growing at a faster rate than any other group even as recorded crime rates are falling overall. While feminists have sought to deal with the consequences of this policy agenda they have been less active in taking a clear position against increased penal control across society more generally (Handler 1992) and in many cases have supported the growth of the carceral state (Snider 1998). This criminalisation of social policy and use of incarceration as a significant mechanism of social control, however, has had devastating effects for many women. It has permitted, Snider argues, an intensification of society's control over women living in poverty, over minorities, native and Aboriginal women. These are the women who bear the heaviest toll of the structural violences which prevail within society. It means too increased surveillance and profiling of women and an increasing tendency to make judgements as to the appropriateness of their individual behaviours. It has invited more racism, stigmatisation and discrimination into their lives, rendering them more vulnerable to social and state harms. It has also increased levels of fear among the population and driven women and girls into the arms of their so-called protectors in a bid to find some amount of safety and security.

The current political climate has seen a restatement of misogyny and violence against women and the election to great political power of a number of people and parties who embody and openly express the worst of these characteristics. This is not a period for tinkering with a broken system but for its replacement. Feminist scholarship can help with this endeavour but only if it retains a strongly critical edge, if it can use its insights to link up with other progressive movements across the globe to internationalise feminist praxis and to ensure that the voices of women are included in their staggering diversity of cultures and practices. We could do worse than to return to more utopian perspectives which contend that fundamental transformation and change in society is possible, which share and raise consciousness internationally in order to reimagine and to reinvent the old ideas of justice and crime upon which we have relied for far too long.

References

Adler, F. (1975) *Sisters in Crime: The Rise of the New Female Criminal*. New York: McGraw Hill.

Barbaret, R. (2014) *Women, Crime and Criminal Justice: A Global Enquiry*. London: Routledge.

Burnett, R. (1992) *The Dynamics of Recidivism*. Oxford: University of Oxford Centre for Criminological Research.

Cain, M. (1990) 'Towards transgression: new directions in feminist criminology', *International Journal of the Sociology of Law*, 18(1): 1–18.

Carlen, P. (1989) 'Feminist prudence – women-wise penology?', *Probation Journal*, 36(3): 110–114.

Carlton, B. and Segrave, M. (eds) (2013) *Women Exiting Prison: Critical Essays on Gender, Post-Release Support and Survival*. London: Routledge.

Carrington, K. (2002) 'Feminism and critical criminology: confronting genealogies', in Carrington, K. and Hogg, R. (eds), *Critical Criminology: Issues, Debates, Challenges*. Cullompton: Willan, pp. 114–142.

Carrington, K. (2015) *Feminism and Global Justice: New Directions in Critical Criminology*. London: Routledge.

Chibber, V. (2016) 'Consent, coercion and resignation: the sources of stability in capitalism', www.youtube.com/watch?v=2dcVoQbhFtQ [Accessed 18 December 2016].

Clarke, R. (2004) *"What Works?" for Women Who Offend. A Service User's Perspective: Exploring the Synthesis between What Women Want and What Women Get*, Research PAPER 2004/4. London: The Griffins Society.

Connell, R.W. (1995) *Masculinities*. Berkeley: University of California Press.

Easton, H., Silvestri, M., Evans, K., Mathews, R. and Walklate, S. (2010) *Evaluation of the Conditional Cautioning Scheme with Referral to Together Women Project Women's Centres*. London: Ministry of Justice.

Faludi, S. (1991) *Backlash: The Undeclared War against American Women*. New York: Crown Publishing.

Farrall, S. (2002) *Rethinking What Works with Offenders: Probation, Social Context and Desistance from Crime*. Cullompton: Willan.

Farrington, D.P. (1997) 'Early prediction of violent and nonviolent youthful offending', *European Journal on Criminal Policy and Research*, 5(2): 51–66.

Fraser, N. (2009) 'Feminism, capitalism and the cunning of history', *New Left Review*, 56: 97–117.

Funk, N. (2013) 'Contra Fraser on feminism and neoliberalism', *Hypatia: A Journal of Feminist Philosophy*, 28(1): 179–196.

Glueck, S. and Glueck, E. (1940) *Juvenile Delinquents Grown Up*. New York: Commonwealth Fund.

Gregory, J. (1986) 'Sex, class and crime: towards a non-sexist criminology', in Matthews, R. (ed), *Confronting Crime*. London: Routledge, pp. 3–53.

Gregory, J. and Lees, S. (1994) 'In search of gender justice: sexual assault and the criminal justice system', *Feminist Review*, 48: 80–93.

Handler, J. (1992) 'Postmodernism, protests and the new social movements', *Law and Society Review*, 26(4): 697–731.

Hanmer, J. (2000) 'Refusing to forget: women's political memories in a comparative perspective', European Feminist Research Conference, 29–30 September, University of Bologna.

Hannah-Moffat, K. (2002) 'Creating choices: reflecting on choices', in Carlen, P. (ed), *Women and Punishment: The Struggle for Justice*. Cullompton: Willan, pp. 199–219.

Hannah-Moffat, K. (2008) 'Re-imaging gendered penalties: the myth of gender-responsivity', in Carlen, P., *Imaginary Penalities*. Cullompton: Willan, pp. 193–217.

Hedderman, C. (2010) 'Government policy on women offenders: Labour's legacy and the coalition's challenge', *Punishment and Society*, 12(4): 485–500.

Hedderman, C., Palmer, E. and Hollin, C. (2008) *Implementing Services for Women Offenders and Those "at Risk" of Offending: Action Research with "Together Women"*, Ministry of Justice Research Series, 12/08. London: Ministry of Justice.

Kimmel, M.S., Hearn, J. and Connell, R.W. (eds) (2005) *Handbook of Studies on Men and Masculinities*. London: Sage.

Lawston, J. and Meiners, E.R. (2014) 'Ending our expertise: feminists, scholarship, and prison abolition', *Feminist Formations*, 26(2): 1–25.

Lee, M. and Haider, S.J. (2012) 'A letter from Bangladesh: developing gender-responsive community policing in Bangladesh', *Crime Prevention and Community Safety*, 14(1): 69–77.

McIvor, G. (2004) *Women Who Offend*. London: Jessica Kingsley.

Maruna, S. (2000) *Making Good: How Ex-Convicts Reform and Rebuild Their Lives*. Washington, DC: American Psychological Association.

Messerschmidt, J. (1997) *Crime as Structured Action: Gender, Race, Class, and Crime in the Making*. Thousand Oaks, CA: Sage.

Naffine, N. (1990) *Law and the Sexes: Explorations in Feminist Jurisprudence*. London: Allen and Unwin.

Radcliffe, P. and Hunter, G. (2016) '"It was a safe place for me to be": accounts of attending women's community services and moving beyond the offender identity', *The British Journal of Criminology*, 56(5): 976–994.

Rex, S. (1999) 'Desistance from offending: experiences of probation', *The Howard Journal of Crime and Justice*, 38(4): 366–383.

Roberts, J. (2010) 'Women offenders: more troubled than troublesome', in Brayford, F., Cowe, B. and Deering, J. (eds), *What Else Works? Creative Work with Offenders.* Cullompton: Willan, pp. 91–116.

Scraton, P. (2016) 'Bearing witness to the "pain of others": researching power, violence and resistance in a women's prison', *International Journal for Crime, Justice and Social Democracy*, 5(1): 5–20.

Segal, L. (1989) 'Slow change or no change? Feminism, socialism and the problem of men', *Feminist Review*, 31: 5–21.

Snider, L. (1998) 'Towards safer societies: punishment, masculinities and violence against women', *The British Journal of Criminology*, 38(1): 1–39.

Trotter, C. (2007) 'Parole and probation', in Sheehan, R., McIvor, G., and Trotter, C. (eds), *What Works with Women Offenders.* Cullompton: Willan, pp. 124–141.

Walklate, S. (1995) *Gender and Crime: An Introduction.* London: Prentice Hall/Harvester Wheatsheaf.

Walklate, S. (2006) *Imagining the Victim of Crime.* Maidenhead: McGraw-Hill/Open University Press.

White, W.L. (2014) 'Advocacy for gender-specific addiction treatment and recovery support: an interview with Dr. Stephanie Covington', www.williamwhitepapers.com/pr/2014%20Dr.%20%20Stephanie%20Covington.pdf [Accessed 2 March 2016].

Williams, L.S., Green, E.L.W. and Williams, K. (2017) 'Trying on gender is the new black: female to felon', in Jackson, S.A. and Gordy, L. (eds), *Through the Prison Gate: An Exploration of Issues from Orange Is the New Black.* London: Routledge.

Index

For Product Safety Concerns and Information please contact our EU
representative GPSR@taylorandfrancis.com
Taylor & Francis Verlag GmbH, Kaufingerstraße 24, 80331 München, Germany

www.ingramcontent.com/pod-product-compliance
Ingram Content Group UK Ltd.
Pitfield, Milton Keynes, MK11 3LW, UK
UKHW011019180926
475701UK00004B/825

* 9 7 8 0 3 6 7 2 2 7 2 1 0 *